Temper Tantrums With God

God

And Other Out of the Box Revelations

By

Jeannie Boatright

Cover Illustration and Design by Rebekah Blair

Published by Truth Rejoices

ISBN: -10:0-9974668-0-4

ISBN-13: 978-0-9974668-0-5

Dedications

First and foremost, I dedicate this book to my wonderful Savior and best friend Jesus Christ. You are my first love and the author and finisher of my faith. May you be glorified!

I dedicate this book to my children Joshua, Shanna, Rebekah, and Caleb. You have always been treasures in my life. I love all of you so very much! Thank you for being such great kids, even in the midst of difficult circumstances. Thank you for your patience and endurance while going through the difficulties of my learning experiences with me. We have shared both triumphs and tragedies. You are all amazing overcomers with incredible destinies!

To Kannesa Baird: Where do I even begin? We have shared so many adventures over the past twenty plus years I couldn't possibly list them. Thank you for your love and support as you walked beside me through both trials and victories. Your prayers and anointing to listen have helped me work through many fears and frustrations and have allowed me to examine the true motives of my heart. You were there through doctor visits, hospital stays, court proceedings, divorce, dating relationships, my daughter's wedding, and even the birth of my first grandchild. At times, when I had no strength, even physically, God's strength flowed through you. We have laughed, cried, and prayed our guts out together. When I moved out of state we both thought distance might distance us, but these past few years, our friendship has continued to flourish in spite of the thousands of miles that have separated us. Thank you for being such a dear friend and sister in Christ!

To Albert Silas: Sometimes God brings people into our lives for a lifetime—sometimes for a season. Thank you for walking with me through an incredibly difficult season. You were always dedicated to my growth as you fought on your knees for my emotional healing and my destiny. You have been a dear friend. I learned so much about my heavenly father's heart through your example. Thank you for pouring so much into my family.

To Rhonda Stone: Sixteen years ago when God brought you into my life I had no idea He had blessed me with such a dear friend, incredible cheerleader, and powerful intercessor. Thank you for burning the midnight oil in prayer for me and for always encouraging me to teach and write the lessons that God has put on my heart.

To Alicia Randall: When I first met you God told me you were a blessing. Thank you for being such a dear friend and neighbor. Not only have you been an incredible encourager, you have an incredible servant's heart. Thank you for visiting me daily when I was stuck in bed writing the majority of this book, and for walking with me though many other fiery trials. I will forever cherish the years during which we shared a walkway and our lives—years filled with love, prayers, laughter, tears, and tons of growth.

To Jan Luke: The moment God divinely brought us together after you shared your testimony at church, I knew that I had been blessed. Soon afterwards you became my first editor. You have been a dear friend and incredible encourager. Thank you for the hours you have spent reading this manuscript, correcting my grammar, and praying for my family. We didn't get to spend much time together before I moved, but I'll never forget our last "God adventure." I'm sure the future holds many more for both of us.

To Lakendra Lewis: From the moment I met you, your infectious smile and bubbly personality brightened my world. I knew in my heart God had blessed me with another lifetime friend. But I had no idea that He had also blessed me with my second editor. The Lord brought us together when you had recently lost your mother, and I was just beginning the journey that would end with the loss of mine. Thank you for joining me on the roller coaster ride these past few years. We have prayed, praised, laughed, and cried together. Thank you for your friendship and for all your professional and godly counsel, as you have read and corrected this manuscript and coached me to birth what God had placed in my heart. I am looking forward to purchasing the first copy of your next book.

To Terry Rendon: I am thankful that God has placed you in my life, not just as an editor, but as a friend. You are a precious young woman and a gifted writer. Your love for the Lord and desire to serve Him is inspiring. Thank you for all of the time you have spent reading and editing.

As I began writing my dedications my mind was flooded with so many precious names and faces of amazing pastors, friends, and family who have prayed for and encouraged my children and me through the years. I decided not to attempt to write them all down, lest I carelessly forget someone. Even though you have not been mentioned by name, I would like all of you to know that your individual fingerprints on my life have been and are still precious to me. I am so very thankful for each and every one of you! May you be abundantly blessed many times over what you have sowed into my life!

Table of Contents

Preface

In 1991, God showed me a vision and told me that I was going to speak and write. I didn't just tell Him "No!" I told Him, "Never!" I had a lot to learn. I thought God was after my obedience. I didn't realize He wanted to capture my heart. Up to that time I had already experienced quite a few "God encounters" in which the Lord had revealed to me that He was my healer, provider, and deliverer, but I had no comprehension of His father's heart. It would take a whole lot more trials and many more revelations for me to begin to understand His love, my value, and the deceptions that kept me in unhealthy relationships.

As God called me out of the boxes of pride, deception, false identity, guilt, rebellion, shame, denial, and fear in which I had been confined, He never condemned me. He just kept loving me. Whether in the midst of a trial, temper tantrum, or victory, He spoke life to me, and revealed His heart for me, bringing truth to my spirit and healing to my wounded soul. In the process, I learned that He is both passionate and compassionate. I also learned that He has a wonderful sense of humor.

The more freedom God brought me, the more my heart longed for others to be free. I couldn't help but share!

I was content with only sharing one-on-one and in

Bible studies. But in 2008, God cleared both my schedule and my excuses to write. I was going through yet another debilitating illness that confined me to my bed. Day and night the revelations that He had brought to me through life experiences (some of them are stories in this book) and corresponding scriptures and studies ran through my head with such intensity I had to write them down. Since I couldn't sit up, a friend loaned me her laptop computer. For weeks I spent every waking hour lying on my back slowly typing with the laptop perched on my chest. I realize now that was all God's goodness. As I gradually recovered I continued to type, and by the time I returned to work three months later, God had birthed the rough drafts of a few books. Since 2008, I have been working on what are now nine books. The second one, *Aha!-More out of the Box Revelations,* should be published by the summer of 2016.

Since the stories in this book are not in chronological order, I have also listed them by topic in the index. No matter how you choose to read this book or portions of it, my purpose in sharing my "temper tantrums" and "out of the box revelations" is to encourage *you* to open *your* mind and heart to receive all God has for *you.* May the Lord abundantly bless you with wisdom and revelation as you experience your own personal *Aha!* moments with Him.

God Speaks

*I*n an instant, years of theological boxes in which I had confined God, were broken. I had heard His voice, and I would never be the same!

Over the past year I had witnessed my beautiful, stately mother take on the resemblance of a prison camp refugee, complete with sunken cheeks and a skeletal appearance. Mom's five foot nine inch frame, reduced to a mere eighty-nine pounds lay draped in organic cotton sheets. Her only room adornments were a super-sized air purifier that hummed 24/7, a neighboring green oxygen tank, and a mid-size television perched on a single dresser a few feet from her bed.

After returning home from being diagnosed with a severe immune system disorder by one of the top clinics in the US, Mom had been confined to the back bedroom of the house, where she survived on organic food flown in from out of town, a container of shots that had to be administered daily, all organic cotton linens and clothes, and her constant companion—her air purifier. She was so highly allergic she couldn't even have visitors in her room. "Not much of a life," I muttered to myself as I peeked around the door for a few minutes to catch a glimpse of her one day before I was heading off to the beach while visiting on spring break. "And it definitely *won't* be mine!"

Years before, when the government outlawed certain pesticides, one of my family members thought it was a waste for the factory where he worked to throw away perfectly good poison. So he sprayed it at our house in order to eliminate our roach problem. The poison was very effective, and we didn't see a live roach for many years. But unfortunately, its long-term effects caused half of my family members to suffer from weakened immune systems and severe central nervous system reactions.

At eighteen, I had already been exhibiting symptoms that were similar to the ones Mom had had at the onset of her infirmity. So that day, as I took in her emaciated frame, I plunged head-first into the river of denial and convinced myself that positive thinking and sheer determination would protect me from a similar fate. But my mind over matter approach did nothing to keep me from the consequences of pesticide poisoning, and I eventually had to swim back to shore and face reality.

By that time, I had been suffering with severe central nervous system problems for almost a year. Although I had frequently experienced loss of muscle control, mild seizures, mini strokes, shortness of breath, and excruciating migraines, I had continued to maintain my "never give up" attitude, telling myself and others "I'll be okay," and refusing to go to the hospital—until the day I found myself staring up at a sea of faces while unable to get up off of the floor of my university's student center. That is when my roommates made an executive decision and drove me a couple of hours to see Mom's doctor. I was immediately admitted to the hospital, where I spent the first of what seemed like an eternity, stuck in a nightmare from which I couldn't awake—a nightmare filled with pain, needles, X-rays, cat scans, tests, and unfamiliar faces.

My nightmare culminated one Wednesday evening when some Swedish specialists were interviewing me and filming my central nervous system reactions. My primary physician informed me that it was a possibility that my Multiple Sclerosis like symptoms could confine me to a wheelchair. "You will never be able to go back home to Corpus Christi, even for a short visit, because of the petrochemicals in the area," he gravely stated. "You will also not be able to return to your university."

I was dumbfounded by the news. When I asked where I could go, the only alternative given was to live in a cabin high in the mountains in a somewhat pure environment. Being a nineteen-year old college student, this was definitely *not* my idea of a future.

I lay in my hospital bed later that night, angrily internally voicing my frustrations to the God I thought only watched over me from a distance: "God, if you are there. I just want you to know this is not fair. Why are you punishing me? I never drank or smoked or slept around. Just so you know, I won't be confined to a wheelchair! And I won't live in some stupid cabin far away from civilization! As a matter-of-fact, I won't live like this—period! I want you to kill me. Just kill me!"

As I inwardly shouted for death, another thought suddenly came to mind. *If God were big enough to **kill** me—then maybe He was big enough to **heal** me!* My focus was then redirected, and the cry of my heart changed course: "Okay, if you are God—then heal me! Just heal me!"

You're probably thinking that I all of a sudden rose up out of my bed miraculously healed and went on with my life, but that is *not* what happened. In the midst of my crying out, I heard a voice so loud it was almost audible speak to my heart as a wave of peace flooded my room: *"Jeannie, if it were meant to be that way, you would not learn what I have for you to learn. Trust me!"* As the words penetrated my spirit, all of the teachings I had received while growing up flooded my mind, and my theological boxes began to break: *God doesn't speak to people anymore.* (But I just heard Him speak.) *Miracles stopped when the last disciple died.* (Why is it that deep inside I feel an assurance that someday I will be healed?) *God is not personally involved in your life.* (But He had just called me by name.) In that moment, the God I thought only watched over me from Heaven had invaded my room, my life, and my heart. Just minutes before I had asked God to end my life, but now, somehow I knew that my life had just begun!

I slept through the night. When I opened my eyes the following morning, not only did I feel lighter inside, I immediately noticed that my motor coordination had improved. Although I hadn't been instantly healed of all of my infirmities, my doctors confirmed that my central nervous system had become more stable, enabling me to complete the battery of tests that were necessary in order to establish the correct doses for the shots I needed to counteract some of my reactions. To everyone's amazement, within a week, I was able to return to my university, although I initially had to do most of my work outside of class.

During my hospital stay I was aware that the student body had been praying for me, but after I returned to campus, I discovered that my Bible study group had been praying for me at the exact time God had spoken to me in my hospital room. This information not only amazed me but made me realize that prayer was more powerful than I had ever imagined.

I could write an entire book about the challenges I faced and the victories I won during the following four years. Since my health was so fragile, I had to stay on a restricted diet, take my shots, sleep on a cotton army cot, and avoid most public gatherings. Thankfully, I was blessed with friends and family who continued to faithfully pray for me. I don't think I would have made it without their prayers. Although, I did have to live in the high mountains that first summer, it wasn't in a cabin, it was in the back of an antique shop in a tiny town in Colorado. After that summer, I still had to be cautious, but I was able to spend longer periods of time in public.

The night God spoke to my heart, He set my feet on a path to discover more about Him—a path leading to exciting adventures with incredible rewards. For in the midst of seemingly insurmountable obstacles, I began to learn how to depend on Him and to hear His voice.

♥ *Heart Encounter* ♥

1. When I returned to campus my teachers agreed to work with me, but they didn't think it would be possible for me to make up the weeks of tests and work I missed while resuming my current studies. Since I could only concentrate for about 10 minutes at a time, I asked the Lord to help me retain information during my short study sessions. With His help, I finished the semester with mostly A's. Besides helping me with my studies, the Lord also began giving me direction in my spirit. "Go here." "Do this." At first, I didn't realize that the nudges were God speaking to me. I believe that was because I equated God's speaking to be as the voice I heard in the hospital. When I finally learned to listen, I realized that God had been speaking to me my whole life. I

just wasn't aware of it. When did you first realize that God was speaking to you?

2. Once I had been witnessing to a friend who called and asked me, "What do you mean when you say God told you something? How does it sound?" I told her that sometimes it's just a thought that's not my own that agrees with God's Word. Sometimes it sounds like a letter being read in my mind. Sometimes it's a nudge or an idea. Sometimes it's a picture with understanding. Sometimes it's a revelation from a Bible passage or confirmation from another person. Rarely, is it the booming almost audible voice. What are some of the ways God has spoken to you?

3. Until my encounter with God in the hospital, I thought God only listened. I didn't believe He spoke. In John 10:27 Jesus says, "My sheep hear My voice." Sheep so distinctly know their shepherd's voice that they answer to it only. Are you learning to distinguish the voice of God?

4. When I started *hearing God*, I mistakenly thought every voice I heard was God's voice. Consequently, I often struggled with deception. We have to learn to discern the difference between our own voice, the

devil's voice, and God's voice. God will not speak something contrary to His Word. He also doesn't condemn or demean. He will convict us, but when He does, He doesn't tear us down. He guides and encourages us. For example: One day God told me I was being selfish in a certain situation. It sounded more like an observation than criticism. But He didn't just leave me there. He said, *"It's okay. I'm going to help you with this."* Can you give an example of a time when God encouraged you and convicted you at the same time?

5. Since I didn't use to believe that God loved me, the devil tormented me on a daily basis. I honestly thought the horrible things the devil was saying to me and about me were from God. Have you ever thought, like I did, that the ugly words the enemy is speaking to you are the voice of God?

6. Read 2 Corinthians 10:3-5. How can these verses help us learn to *hear God* over the interference of the enemy and of our flesh?

7. Are you taking your thoughts captive? When I first began to take my thoughts captive, I had to write down what I was hearing. Seeing my thought life on

paper helped me to better recognize what did or did not line up with the Word and God's heart. The first statement I examined was a remark I had often heard during my marriage. After writing down, "No one wants to hear anything you have to say," I was confused as to what the truth would be. Surely, it wasn't "Everyone *wants* to hear what you have to say." When I asked God to give me truth He told me, "It doesn't matter as long as you say what I tell you to say." That revelation was the beginning of the breaking off of many lies in my life. Can you relate? What are some of the lies you have either believed in the past or are currently believing?

8. Not only did I have to learn to discern truth from lies, I also had to learn to pay attention to how what I heard affected my emotions. Making impulsive decisions when I thought I was hearing from God almost always proved to be disastrous (Like the time I ran to the other side of the church to meet the grandmother of the man I thought God just told me would be my future husband.). Have you ever, like me, made decisions based on extreme emotions, thinking it was God's direction? Explain.

On the following page is a list of comparisons a friend posted on the Internet that have helped me to better discern God's voice. I pray this list will bless you as it has me:

God's Voice	Satan's Voice
Stills you	*Rushes you*
Leads you	*Pushes you*
Reassures you	*Frightens you*
Enlightens you	*Confuses you*
Encourages you	*Discourages you*
Comforts you	*Worries you*
Calms you	*Obsesses you*
Convicts you	*Condemns you*

Psalm 86:6 says: "Give ear, O Lord, to my prayer; and attend to the voice of my supplications. In the day of my trouble I will call upon You, for You will answer me." God answered me when I called. Although it would take years for me to understand His love, the night God spoke to me in my hospital room I realized He was a whole lot bigger and more involved in my life than I had imagined. Four years later, He answered the second prayer I prayed that night in the hospital. After having a couple of prophetic dreams, I agreed to go to a charismatic Bible study with some friends. When the group leaders anointed me and prayed over me I was

miraculously healed. That night I threw away $1,000 worth of medication and stepped into a brand new life. Six months later my mother was healed through a word of knowledge while watching the 700 Club. Again, God had spoken, but not just to hearts—to mountains!

Let's Pray:

Dear Lord, I am so grateful that you answer when I call. Thank you for caring for me so much that you desire to speak to my heart. Open my ears so I can hear your voice. Help me to discern your voice from the voice of the enemy and from the voice of my own desires. Thank you, dear Shepherd, for faithfully leading and guiding me. In Jesus' Name...Amen!

Reflections:

My Father's Eyes

Once when I was praying for a battered woman to have a revelation of God's love, I saw a picture of small drab squares of material in her head. As I continued to pray for her, the Lord told me that the pieces of material were quilt squares that represented bits of *head knowledge* that needed to be transformed through revelation and sewed in her heart. Although, at the time, I had some understanding of what God was showing me, the message really *hit home* one afternoon when I was babysitting my good friend's daughter.

The *little darling* was a strong-willed, wide-eyed, brunette who was at the height of her terrible twos. Needless to say she was a bit of a challenge. After one particular trying morning of continuous temper tantrums, she fell asleep in my arms. Not only had she exhausted herself, but me as well. I remember thinking, as I held the toddler, "Thank God she is asleep!" About that time her father arrived.

After coming in the house and taking a few steps into

the room, He threw his hands up in the air and sighed. Then he came over to the couch where I was holding his child. I watched in stunned silence as he knelt and reached over and touched his daughter's face. With an expression of awe and adoration he whispered, "Isn't she beautiful?! Isn't she just beautiful?!"

"Beautiful? I thought to myself. "What is he talking about? She's a little terror!" I watched his fingers gently caress his daughter's cheek. Then I raised my eyes and studied his face. His tender expression of adoration both confused and captivated me. I felt a stirring in the depths of my soul. Then I saw a glimpse of his heart for his daughter. When I looked back down at his daughter's face, I saw her through her daddy's eyes. She was absolutely beautiful! I was still trying to take it all in, when my Father God tenderly spoke to my spirit, "*That's how I see you.*"

In that instant a significant part of my childhood was re-written. Images of the disappointment on my father's face and the frustration in his words to me were shattered. I was no longer the little girl who couldn't "do enough" or "be good enough." I was now "the adored one," God's beautiful child. It was as if God went into my head and found the little drab piece of cloth that I had stored away—the one labeled "Loving Father," pierced it with the needle of truth and transformed it into a piece of the finest silk. Then He moved it from my head and gently sewed it to a quilt of love that was being pieced together in my heart. "Head knowledge" had become "heart knowledge," and my *Father God* had become *Daddy* the afternoon I saw both a little child and myself through my "Father's Eyes."

I grew up believing that God was distant and disconnected. Although I was aware He saved me from my sins, I really didn't believe that He *knew* me or even *liked* me— much less *adored* me. It took many years and many revelations, like the one I just shared, for Him to convince me otherwise. But His loving persistence paid off, and I can now honestly say that I am not only known, but loved and adored by my *Heavenly Daddy!*

♥ *Heart Encounter* ♥

1. How about you? Do you believe that God adores you and sees you as beautiful? Why or why not?

2. It wasn't just the words my friend spoke to his daughter that touched my heart. It was also his expression. He looked at her as if she were a work of art. She was, and so are you! Do you believe you are God's masterpiece?

3. Although my father loved his family, since he was rather controlling and critical, I saw God as being the

same. I didn't understand my value because I didn't "feel" I could ever "measure up" to my earthly father's nor my Heavenly Father's expectations. What was or is your father like? How do you view your Heavenly Father?

4. I often talk to people about the *father wound*. But this past year I have met many people with *mother wounds*. I'm beginning to realize both wounds, not only affect the way we view ourselves and God, but they also affect our relationships. Have your relationships been affected by *father or mother wounds*? If so, how?

5. In Romans 8:15, Paul uses the term "Abba Father" to describe our relationship with God. The Strong's Concordance tells us that Abba is also used as the term of *tender endearment* by a beloved child. It describes an *affectionate, dependent relationship* with the child's father, *daddy* or *papa*. In the story, I mentioned that *Father God* became *Daddy*. To me the word *father* denotes authority or relational position, but *Daddy* speaks of passion. Do you believe that God is passionate about you? In *your* heart has He become your *Abba Daddy?*

As I mentioned earlier, it took years and many revelations for me to understand God's heart for me. Without his being aware, my earthy father ended up participating in some of those revelatory moments. A few years ago I had the privilege of sharing with my father, not just my childhood pain, but the revelation and restoration God has brought me. Now that God has brought more healing to both of us, praise God, I have an earthly *Daddy* as well as a *Heavenly Daddy*.

Let's Pray:

Daddy God, thank you for the beautiful quilt you are sewing in my heart. Continue to renew my mind with the Word and with your words of healing, as you bring me revelation and change my "head knowledge" to "heart knowledge." Show me how my relationships with my earthly father and mother have affected my relationship with you and others. Thank you for loving me. I know you are passionate about me. I want to be passionate about you! I love you, Lord! In Jesus' Name…..Amen!

Reflections:

_____

_____

_____

_____

_____

_____

_____

_____

_____

Trash

Since our precious Lord often uses "weak and foolish things" to confound the wise (or so we think ourselves to be at times), sometimes His rhema words, or revelations that penetrate our spirits, come in the midst of the most unlikely situations. Such was the case in my life one afternoon in the early 1990's, when I had been diligently searching for a small horseshoe magnet that I had set aside for some of our home school experiments.

Earlier in the morning everything had been running like clockwork. I had cleared the dishes from lunch and began to transfer the science materials from the counter top to the table, which was encircled by my wide-eyed preschool and primary age children. I could sense their excitement mounting each time I placed another item in front of them. But when I reached for the "star of the show"—the powerful little horseshoe—to my surprise, it was nowhere to be found!

Upon discovering the magnet was missing, I began

the "mommy inquisition." You know, the one that starts out with a gentle trill of, "Has anyone seen Mommy's magnet?" and progresses to forceful threats of intimidation, dire consequences, and eternal grounding if the missing item is "not returned—IMMEDIATELY!" However, it didn't take long for me to realize by the stupefied looks on the faces of my children that they were not the culprits. I then turned to plan B—a search.

After momentarily dismissing the children, I began to hastily rearrange the items on the counter and scan the kitchen floor when the Lord spoke to my heart: *"It's in the trash."* Since I realized that this could be an unwelcome but logical possibility, I scooted a chair over next to the trash can, positioned myself for the unpleasant chore in front of me, and meticulously began lifting off the top layers. After I had removed only a few items I heard: *"Not in **that** trash."*

"Wait a minute, Lord," I inwardly objected, "This is the only trash I have!" Rationalizing that I must have "misheard" God, I chose to ignore the instruction and began digging through the trash more fervently than before. But after plucking out a few fragrant diapers and slimy garbage disposal rejects with still no magnet in site, I heard in my spirit yet again, *"It's not in **that** trash."*

This time I paused for a minute or two in order to analyze the current situation (of course, not asking for wisdom) and with no apparent solution in sight, confusion enveloped me like a cloud. The two messages I had been given seemed to conflict with each other. So I decided to dismiss any attempt at understanding and continued to move forward by donning plastic bags to form makeshift gloves in order to avoid the really gooey, gross stuff I knew would be awaiting me near the bottom of the can.

Now, being fully armed for the task at hand, I sat back down and resumed my mission. However, as I reached further into the garbage, I heard the still small voice of the Lord repeat a third time, *"It's not in **that** trash."*

Once again, instead of stopping and asking the Lord what He was trying to tell me, I resumed my standoff. There was a reason why He kept telling me to look up the scripture about not being stubborn like the mule in those days. Nothing was making sense, and I was a woman on a mission. "Come hell or high water," I was determined to find that magnet; no matter what—even if it killed me! Thus, in a final act of defiance and assured victory, I picked up the trash can and dumped all of its remaining contents on the floor. After sifting through the debris and still coming up empty-handed, I found myself in a stalemate.

I hate to admit it now, but in those days when the Lord told me to do something, I thought I had the option of how I would respond. After listening to the instruction, I would ponder it for a moment or two, and then give Him my decision, which depending on the request, would either be "yes," "no," "maybe," or "absolutely no way—

ever!" I have since purposed to never say "never," for I believe saying "never" to God is the same as a toddler saying he can rule the world. It doesn't make sense! From too many experiences to relate, I have learned that my "nevers" in heaven's language are interpreted as "definitely yes," after God has let me go around the mountain umpteen times and worked enough *self* out of me to get me to do what He asked me to do in the *first* place. Take my word for it, it's easier to just say "yes" the first time.

Because I didn't understand rebellion during this season of my life, I viewed obedience more like a little child selecting ice cream. Since there were some flavors I liked and some I disdained, certainly, God did not intend for me to choose the ones I loathed. In reality, I was blinded by foolishness and pride, and was under the deception that if I knew more of what God knew, I could be free of temptation and sin forever. I hated battling my flesh, and I was convinced that the scripture "be perfect even as I am perfect" could be worked out in my life if I just *knew* more. This is a self-righteous interstate to nowhere. Take my advice—don't even get on the access road!

So, bound by deception and covered with confusion, I sat on the floor with trash all around me wondering what had gone wrong. Finally, I threw up my hands in exasperation and exclaimed, "I give up!!!" Thankfully, since surrender and victory are the same in the eyes of God, I was ready for a teachable moment. And as soon as

I quieted myself and asked God for wisdom, I *instantly* knew where the magnet was located.

I pulled off my makeshift gloves and reached under the refrigerator. Sure enough, clinging to the metal in a small pile of trash, was my magnet. As I took hold of it, I heard very clearly (and this time it was not a small voice), *"You will never understand me! Quit trying to figure me out!"* Isaiah 55: 8-9 which talks about God's ways not being mine, came to mind, and I was humbled by this revelation from my Holy God!

Although God loves us and knows what is best for us, how many times do we continue to dig through the "trash of life" because we are too stubborn to stop and listen and obey His counsel? Just think of all of the disgusting things I could have been spared had I not dug through the trash that day, as well as many other times in my life. It would have been so much easier if I had only learned to surrender and listen sooner. The sad thing is, for years, I wasn't even aware I was rebellious because I thought rebellion was only outward. I focused so much on trying to be a "good girl," by living a moral life and doing the "right things" for God, that I was blinded to the true condition of my heart.

It says in 1 Samuel 16:7 "...For *the Lord does* not *see* as man sees; for man looks at the outward appearance, but the Lord looks at the heart."

David says in Psalm 139:23&24 "Search me, O God, and know my heart: Try me, and know my anxieties; And see if *there is any* wicked way in me. And lead me in the way everlasting." When I first allowed God to show me what was in my heart, I discovered that I had often done the *right* things while operating out of *wrong* motives. I didn't recognize my rebellion because it was hidden so well, taking on the camouflage of self-dependence, self-righteousness, or a myriad of other disguises. Unveiling my rebellion helped me become more sensitive to the Holy Spirit, which resulted in me making some serious changes in both my attitude and actions—releasing me to receive more blessings.

♥ *Heart Encounter* ♥

1. In 1 Samuel 15:23 when Saul had the kingdom torn from him because of his rebellion, the prophet Samuel told him, "rebellion *is as* the sin of witchcraft." What do you think? Do you think that this is a harsh comparison? Why or why not?

2. I used to think this comparison was harsh, but after interceding for both people choosing blatant rebellion and those operating in witchcraft, I have become aware of definite parallels. Both rebellion and witchcraft operate out of a spirit of control, such as: "I will control my own life, and if possible I will also control the lives of others." Both rebellion and

witchcraft also operate out of deception and pride. And both rebellion and witchcraft open us up to the voice of the enemy and keep us from hearing the voice of God. With these things in mind do you think as children of God we should take rebellion seriously? Explain.

3. Have you asked the Lord to show you if you have rebellion in your heart? If so, how do you see it manifesting in your thoughts and actions?

4. Examine your thoughts when your plans don't work or when you face other disappointments. If you are like me, the first phrase that goes through your mind is probably not "Praise Jesus!" Have you ever kept a record of your self-talk throughout the course of a day? If not, I challenge you to try it to see what patterns routinely show up in your thinking.

5. The Bible tells us that our mouths speak from the abundance of what is in our hearts (Luke 6:45). Listen to what is coming out of your mouth. What do you find yourself saying in the midst of frustrating situations?

6. Have you ever considered some of the motives behind your actions? I have often discovered that some of my good deeds or right actions were to seek approval or pacify guilt instead of just to glorify God. Ask the Lord to reveal to you if there might be some wrong heart motivations behind any of your actions. Write down anything that comes to mind.

God is love, and He wants us to seek and know His heart. I didn't have a concept of His love, so instead I sought to know His actions. Since I didn't trust God, I tried to rely on my own understanding and control what I didn't know. I thought if I could just understand what God was doing, I could trust Him more. However, I have learned the opposite is true. The more I understand His heart for me, the more I *do* trust Him.

Let's Pray:

Precious Lord, you know all things. You know my heart better than I could ever know it myself. Lord, I want my heart to become totally devoted to you so I can honor you with my life and in my actions. Shine the light of your Holy Spirit and show me my inward rebellion. Illuminate the hidden things that I may not have wanted to see. Remind me, as in Psalms 139, that you search me and know me, and that you also know my thoughts from afar. Lord, forgive me for trying to live areas of my life apart from you. Forgive me for the times when I have tried "to figure things out" on my own. When you ask something of me, my only response should be, "Yes, Lord." Sweet Jesus, forgive me for all the times I have answered otherwise. I want to serve you. Keep growing me and changing me more into your image. I love you, Lord! In Jesus' Name...Amen!

Reflections:

_____

_____

_____

_____

_____

_____

_____

More Than a Piano

Since our Heavenly Father not only knows our needs, but also our desires, He will sometimes drop blessings in our laps when we least expect them. That is exactly what He did when He was bringing me truth and freedom concerning my warped image of Father God.

Like so many people, my image of God was one of a relationally distant authoritarian whom I could never please. I was always walking a fine line. If I made right choices, I thought that God would tolerate me. But when I made wrong choices, I would frantically glance up waiting for lightning to strike. Even on my best days, I couldn't comprehend a smile coming from heaven's direction.

I worshiped God because He was powerful. I also acknowledged Him as my Healer (Jehovah Rapha) as well as my Provider (Jehovah Jireh) because I had experienced both firsthand. But it never once dawned on me that God loved me, or that He might want to give me the desires of my heart—especially since I thought desiring things was selfish, and selfishness was sin.

That is why I was amazed when the Lord blessed us with a house! Our family of six had become quite cramped in our small apartment. When I began to pray for a larger place to rent, I never imagined that God would stir the hearts of a couple we barely knew to *give* us a down payment for a house! Although I was excited and thankful for the incredible blessing, since back then I still believed that I had to somehow earn God's approval and blessings, I struggled with receiving the gift. I couldn't understand it. "Why would God give us a house?" I questioned. After brainstorming the possibilities, I settled on the most unselfish reason I could think of: God needs us in a certain house because I am supposed to share Jesus in a new neighborhood. My conclusion relieved my guilt and enabled me to make the move.

Shortly after moving into our house, I took the children over to visit a friend who also had recently moved. As she was giving us a tour of her new home I noticed a piano nestled in a little alcove. It was very old and in disrepair. As my eyes scrolled down its ivory keys, a flicker of longing stirred in my heart. A longing I knew it was impossible to satiate.

For the rest of the day, I had difficulty concentrating. I just couldn't get the piano out of my mind. I tried to squelch the yearning, but it was futile. I might as well have been trying to put out a forest fire with a cup of water. I realized this desire for a piano had been in my heart since childhood.

My mother had inherited her mother's piano when I was five. The beautiful melodies that flowed from its ivory and ebony keys caressed me as I lay in my bed at night listening to her play from the living room. As I grew older, I began making up worship songs and would sometimes sit for hours awkwardly plunking them out on the keyboard. Eventually, I was presented with piano lessons, but I became frustrated and quit—a decision I have always regretted.

After seeing my friend's piano that afternoon, a mixture of both current longing and past regret caused me to pray a desperate prayer. "Lord, remove this desire if it is not *Your* will and bring it to pass if it is!" I honestly thought that God would remove the desire because it seemed ridiculous that He would want me to have something so unnecessary and expensive. That is why I was stunned when I heard in my heart, *"I am sending you a piano."* Although I was both amazed and thrilled, when I considered my present circumstances, I figured it would be at least ten years before I would see the promise fulfilled. I think God was smiling.

A few months later, my folks came out to visit. Since Dad and Mom had made it a ritual to attend the annual automotive swap meet in California almost every fall, we could usually expect a visit either before or after the event. This particular year, it was after. The morning after their arrival, Dad walked in with a newspaper and asked me if I wanted to go check out some yard sales. He then proceeded to show me a yard sale ad listing a piano and asked if I would like to go look at it. My jaw dropped. I had told no one of the promise God had given me, and quite frankly, I didn't know what to do. I was afraid of manipulating the situation and *making* something happen, but Dad was so persistent, I reluctantly agreed to go.

The entire drive over, excitement, unworthiness, apprehension, and desire all sparred against each other in my mind, and there was no victor by the time we arrived at the house.

The owner, a stylish woman appearing to be in her late sixties, ushered us into an elegant dining room. Sitting in the corner was a lovely piano. Instead of being worn and in disrepair as I imagined, its beautiful maple wood casing gleamed in the dim light. My heart was racing. "It's so beautiful," I thought to myself, "is it going to be mine? She must be asking at least $200." I started to get excited.

"How much do you want for the piano?" Dad questioned in his baritone voice.

"I am asking $600," the woman softly answered.

"$600!" I internally lamented, "I knew it had to have been too good to be true!" I waited for Dad to turn around and walk away. But, to my surprise, Dad didn't even shake his head.

Since, to me, $600 was a substantial sum, my poverty spirit manifested. So I decided to test the situation. I asked the woman why she was selling her piano. When she explained that her hands had become too arthritic to play, I tried to convince her to keep it anyway. Dad was probably wondering what on earth I was doing, but since an impractical gift of this proportion was way out of my comfort zone, I really wanted God to prove to me that He was in this.

Despite my coaxing, the woman still remained adamant about selling. That is when Dad motioned for me to go outside. Once outside, he pulled me aside and said, "Do you want the piano?" Then he proceeded to inform me: "The swap meet got rained out so I didn't spend the money I brought. If you want the piano I'm going to offer her $400."

A swirl of emotions swarmed inside me. Could this be God? I quickly ran the events leading up to this moment through my head: God promised a piano. I never told anyone. Dad finds the ad. Dad wants to look at the piano. I couldn't talk the lady into keeping the piano. The swap meet got rained out. Dad wants to buy the piano. It wouldn't take a rocket scientist to figure out *it was God.* So the verdict was in, the offer was accepted, and the piano became mine.

Although I never learned to play it well, that piano ended up being a gift that kept on giving. It brought me joy, encouraged me to be creative, and comforted me through many difficult times. I eventually passed it on to one of my daughters.

The beautiful maple wood piano is no longer in my house, but it still is, and forever will be, in my heart—

reminding me that a "father's heart is to bless." I will always cherish the day when My Father God gave me the desires of my heart through my earthly father. And I'm not just talking about the piano.

♥ Heart Encounter ♥

1. What are some desires that are buried deep in your heart? How do those desires sometimes manifest outwardly?

2. The gift of the piano satisfied a longing, but how it was gifted answered a heart cry. I have learned that often when I desire something in the natural, there is a hidden heart cry that is longing to be nurtured. Can you think of a situation in your life when this has been the case?

3. Psalm 21:1-3 states, "THE KING [David] shall joy in your strength, Oh Lord; and in your salvation how greatly shall he rejoice! You have given him his heart's desire and have not withheld the requests of his lips..." (AMP). When David wrote this Psalm he obviously was aware that God gives heart's desires.

Do you believe that God wants to give you the desires of your heart? Why or why not?

4. Matthew 7:9 talks about how God gives good gifts: "Or what man is there among you who, if his son asks for bread, will give him a stone? Or if he asks for a fish, will he give him a serpent? If you then, being evil, know how to give good gifts to your children, how much more will your Father who is in heaven give good things to those who ask Him?" As parents desire to give blessings to their children, our Heavenly Father desires to give to us. However, I can recall times when what I desired would not have been what was best for me. Although I might have been asking for what looked to me like bread or fish, God in His wisdom knew that my request was really a stone or serpent. I am now very thankful that those desires were not given to me. Have you ever been thankful for unanswered prayers? Explain.

Psalm 37:4 says to "Delight yourself also in the Lord, and He will give you the desires *and* secret petitions of your heart" (AMP). I am so thankful that God loves us and He knows us better than we know ourselves. I didn't expect my father to buy me a piano, but God knew that my father's purchasing the piano would both give me a physical blessing and apply some healing balm to my earthly father wound. As you and I place our trust in God, we can be confident that He will fulfill our "true" heart's desires—maybe not in the ways we expected, but in the ways they will be most accepted.

Let's Pray:

Dear Lord, you know the true desires of my heart. I lay down my own ideas and expectations and trust that you will bring to pass every good thing you have for me. You are a loving father who knows the difference between bread and stones. Thank you for choosing what is best for me and orchestrating the circumstances that are necessary to fulfill my heart's desires. In Jesus' Name….Amen!

Reflections:

_____
_____
_____
_____
_____
_____
_____
_____
_____

Not Your Cup

Although it had been such a short while ago, the memories were already beginning to fade. Just weeks before I had witnessed the supernatural love of God touch thousands of lives, and now, I was once again stuck in bed for an indeterminate amount of time.

After passing out in the Hong Kong airport coming home from the mission field, I had been taken by wheelchair for the rest of the returning flights. Within a few days of my homecoming I was transported by ambulance to the hospital. Now, having been released with a long list of specialists with which to follow up, I was exhausted, overwhelmed, and aggravated. I was also incredibly weak. Since my brain had some kind of disconnect which caused my eyes to roll back in my head and my body to collapse like a rag doll if I tried to sit or stand for more than a minute, even a simple trip to the bathroom meant some time on the floor. But this particular day it wasn't what I couldn't do that had me so upset—it was what I couldn't be—or more specifically, what I didn't look like anymore.

"You're beautiful!"

Maybe it was because I was an American; maybe it was because I resembled *someone*. But whatever the reason, as our AGLOW International team ministered in the various *barangays*, or small villages, my Filipino brothers' and sisters' kind words had touched a place in my heart—making me feel—well—*beautiful*. But that had not always been the case.

Due to verbal and emotional abuse, the word *beautiful* used to be the last word I would have used to describe myself. However, over a period of time during which God had graciously brought healing to my broken heart, I had taken on a new identity. I had become aware of God's unconditional love for me, grown in confidence, gained some very necessary weight, learned to be more assertive, developed healthier boundaries, and enjoyed receiving compliments almost daily. Life was good, and most of the time, I liked who I was.

However, this particular morning, as I once again lamented the loss of my appearance, the old tapes of the enemy began to play in my head: "You are so ugly!" "No one would ever want you!" "You have nothing to give anyone!" Although I knew I shouldn't be in agreement with these thoughts, I looked down at my loose skin, which seemed to affirm what I was hearing. I had already lost quite a bit of weight, and my coloring fluctuated between white and pale gray. And to top it off, there was a cup with my picture on it resting on the shelf beside my bed that confirmed my resolution.

Once again, I looked over at the horrible picture. It was clearly my face—pale and misshapen with sunken eyes staring back at me. The cup had been given to me as a gift by the team on one of the islands where we ministered. Weeks before the trip each team member sent in a picture. Since I was having difficulty finding a photo, I had a friend take a quick snapshot and sent it off. At the time, I thought, "What a terrible picture, but, oh well!" Little did I know that the picture would be displayed along with those of the other team members at the three-day conference that culminated our trip. Not only was it a terrible picture to begin with, but after it had been shrunk horizontally so it would fit in the allotted space on the conference poster, my face looked as if it had been caught in an elevator door. I laughed along with the others when I saw it, but inside there was a pang of grief—and identification.

Now the cup bearing the same picture that was presented to me as a token of appreciation was a constant reminder that I was no longer beautiful. As I turned away in disgust and attempted to focus on other things, my sister Nancy called to say she was stopping by. A little while later, she approached my bed holding a brown paper bag and said, "God told me to go to an antique store and buy you a gift." I fully expected her to give me a token with a scripture or a shepherd on it that said: "Yea, though I walk through the valley of the shadow of death…" But instead she continued to clutch the bag and share the details of her shopping trip.

Apparently, the Lord had told Nancy to go to a particular antique store. When she looked around the store, nothing jumped out at her, so she had asked the Lord what she was looking for. The Holy Spirit then revealed to her that she was looking for a broken cup.

My eyes stayed fixed on my sister as she paused long enough to reach down into her bag. I envisioned her withdrawing shattered pieces of ceramic or china as I thought to myself, "Lord, I'm not that much of a mess, am I?" But both to my relief and surprise, she pulled out a delicate miniature teacup and placed it in my hand.

As I admired its lovely floral pattern and scalloped gold edges, Nancy continued on with her story. Upon further exploration, the Lord had told her that she was looking for a beautiful cup with the vessel intact, but with the handle missing. Since she couldn't find an item fitting that description, she approached the counter and asked the owner if she had a cup with a missing handle. Receiving a quizzical expression from the woman in response, Nancy went on to tell her, "My sister is very sick, and the Lord told me to come in and buy her a cup with a broken handle." I thought to myself, "Wow! Now that's boldness! GO SIS!" At that point, the owner slowly nodded her head and took a tiny cup, about the size of a silver dollar, from the curio cabinet in front of the register. "It was so beautiful," exclaimed the owner, "that I just couldn't bear to throw it away!"

I started to tear up as I thought about how God hadn't

thrown *me* away, either. As I continued to examine the intricate vessel, my sister told me, "You are beautiful and intact, but there is a fracture that God wants to heal." Then after a brief pause, Nancy reached into the bag once more while mentioning, "There is another part." She then handed me something wrapped in tissue. As I peeled back the paper to reveal the matching saucer, she commented, "God told me you would know what it stood for." The saucer spoke to me of hope and restoration. I immediately blurted out, "It's the double portion!"

Before she left, Nancy said the Lord was going to send other people to speak to me about the cup. After her departure, I continued to turn it in my hands and scrutinize the details. The cup appeared to be hand painted. It's pink, orange, and green full petal flowers were each outlined in gold and a raised beaded design surrounded its base. However, it wasn't the cup's design that first caught my attention. It was the number 49 that was taped inside just below the edge,. Ever since I had learned that the number 7 represents restoration, seven sevens or 49 had spoken to me of seven-fold restoration. So my spirit leapt when I saw it. Later on, after looking at the receipt, I would also become aware that the cup and saucer were purchased on April 9th or 4/9.

But it was what was printed under the item number that struck a chord with the pain in my heart. In small letters in parenthesis were the words *"as is."* Those two little words reminded me of God's love in a big way. Yes, God loves me *as is*. His love and adoration are not contingent on having my stuff together or looking a certain way. In His eyes I am cherished and beautiful—no matter what I look like or in what condition I am.

Not long after my sister's departure, my good friend Kannesa came over to take care of me for a while. Since I was unable to write, I asked her to jot down some brief statements concerning the cup. As Kannesa was writing, she looked up and said, "Jeannie, the gold details in the flowers remind me of the Holy Spirit in your life. God wants you to see your beauty. Do you mind if I read something to you?" Then she read me a few passages from Staci and John Eldridge's book, *Captivating*. Although, God had ministered to me powerfully when I read the book and taught a subsequent Bible study from it a few years earlier, I found myself receiving portions of the book like fresh manna.

It had been easier to feel captivating when I thought I was *looking good*, but now I was back to believing *by faith*. I had to seriously ask myself why I was basing my beauty on my looks. About that time, Janet, my team leader from our mission's trip called. She, as well as many others, had been praying for me; she was checking on my progress. I told her the story of the cup. I explained to her that although I knew that *God* saw me as beautiful, I felt disgusting and ugly at that moment since I had lost quite a bit of weight and had the coloring of a corpse.

Janet pointed out that the cup had no handle because we are always trying to find something to grab hold of, whether it is our looks, our income, our position, or our talents. Then she told me that I needed to fast how I saw myself. Since the word fast usually connotes giving up eating, she clarified, "Don't fast food! Fast how *you see yourself*, until you see yourself how *God* sees you!" I knew she was right. I needed to starve my negative thinking. It wasn't good enough to know that *God* saw me as beautiful. *I* also had to see my beauty. Before she hung up, Janet prayed for both my emotional and physical healing.

Later that evening, my dear friend Rhonda stopped by. When I shared the story of the cup with her, she said, "Tiny cups like that aren't usually picked up by their handles. You have to take hold of the whole thing. I think God is trying to tell you that you need to embrace your whole self."

During the next few days, the Lord continued to minister to some deep wounds in my soul through the cup and through other Christian brothers and sisters. Then He sent Nancy back again. This time her husband Jerry was with her. Together, they were holding another bag containing a different cup. But this time instead of bringing forth a treasure to minister to me, the bag was lowered and they helped me hold a hammer. As the hammer repeatedly crashed down on the bag, the Lord spoke to my heart, *"THAT'S NOT YOUR CUP!"* When we were through, the cup with my distorted picture on it, along with the lies which I had been believing was smashed into a myriad of tiny pieces.

It's much easier for us to see ourselves as beautiful when we are looking our *best*. But often, how we truly view ourselves is revealed when we are at our *worst*. God does not question our beauty. Since we are His beloved, He always sees us as beautiful. The question is: What do we see?

Each day is full of choices. One of those choices is how we see ourselves. We can either see ourselves through God's eyes or through the enemy's lies. Two cups are held out in front of you. One is a cup of reality representing your true beauty. Take hold of it. Wrap your hands around it, and accept your whole self *as is*. The other one has a distorted image. Reject it and smash it with the hammer of truth—for that is **NOT YOUR CUP!**

♥ *Heart Encounter* ♥

1. How do you see yourself?

2. Are you accepting a cup of lies or receiving truth?

3. Does your image of yourself change according to how you view your external appearance, i.e., weight, wrinkles, etc?

4. Proverbs 31:30 says that "Charm *and* grace are deceptive, and beauty is in vain [because it is not lasting], but a woman who reverently *and* worshipfully fears the Lord, she shall be praised!" (AMP). Do you agree or disagree? Why or why not?

5. *"Beauty is in the eye of the beholder"* might be a familiar phrase, but it's true. What is beautiful to one person or a culture may not be beautiful to another. What is your standard for judging beauty? Do you find yourself defining beauty according to the images presented in the media and/or others' opinions, or is your definition of beauty based on the truth of God's Word?

6. Read Genesis 1:26-31. God is the God of completion. When man and woman were created, the creation was complete. Why do you think the Word says that God said, *"It is very good"* after the creation of Adam and Eve?

7. Verse 27 says, "So God created man in his *own* image; in the image of God He created him; male and female He created them." What does it mean to be made in the image of God? How should knowing we

are made in God's image affect the way you and I see, think, and feel about ourselves?

8. What does 1 Peter 3:3-4 reveal about true beauty?

9. Although beauty as it is mentioned in this passage relates to women, I believe that beauty in God's view is neither masculine nor feminine. What do you think?

There was a time when I was very angry with a man who was making terrible decisions. When I was praying, I felt that God was going to show me how to love him. The next time I saw this man, not only did I see his sin separate from his person, my spiritual eyes were opened and I saw him as the most beautiful creature I had ever laid eyes upon. It was such an incredible revelation of how God sees you and me as being beautiful, that if I could combine the most beautiful sunsets, the grandest mountains, and the deepest oceans into one single work of art, it would not compare to the glimpse God gave me of what He sees when He looks at us.

When I was in junior high there was a poster in my Sunday school room that said "God Don't Make Junk." Well He doesn't, even if there are times we feel as though there might be an exception where we are concerned. You and I are created in the image of God to reflect His glory. When the Lord looks at us He sees His beautiful child, NO EXCEPTIONS!

A good friend of mine recently shared a story with me about a woman who was having a difficult time accepting herself. He shared that this woman's husband told her to let him be her mirror. Isn't that what God says to us? "*It doesn't matter what you see. Let **Me** be your mirror and show you what **I** see.*" What a precious husband! What a precious Heavenly Father!

Let's Pray:

Lord, I thank you that I am beautiful, and the beauty that you have given me cannot be altered or marred. Forgive me for the times I have accepted a warped image of myself. Help me to embrace my entire self as you so lovingly embrace all of me. Break the cup of lies telling me that I am not beautiful, and help me to fast how I see myself until I see what you see. I continue to declare freedom and victory over every area of my life. Sweet Jesus, be my mirror, and always remind me that the most beautiful reflection of me will always be the reflection of you in my life. In Jesus' Name…Amen!

Reflections:

_____
_____
_____
_____
_____
_____
_____
_____
_____

Clearer Vision

I used to be a member of the CGWA—***Closet Glasses Wearers of America***. Except for driving, my insecurities kept my face pretty much frame free. However, since he who sees little can't deal with life normally, I constantly had to adjust my lifestyle, which included gravitating to the front of classrooms and church pews and ordering fast food using the buddy system. I also trained myself to recognize approaching friends by their height, build, and hair color instead of their facial features.

For the most part, my little system worked pretty well for me. However, there were the occasional embarrassing slips, such as when I would flag down total strangers in the grocery store thinking they were acquaintances, or when I would be accused of snobbery after supposedly ignoring someone I knew in passing. Incidences such as these called for either extreme creativity or total humiliation. I ended up mastering in both.

Since my vision continued to get worse I knew I

would eventually have to convert to contacts or "change my vain ways." So the morning I discovered the metal art project my toddler created after discovering my glasses on the coffee table, I made an appointment for an eye exam to get contacts. While I was getting ready to leave the house, I had a little nudge in my spirit that something wasn't quite right. I learned later from a friend the "no peace, no purchase rule," but since I was so set on saying goodbye to my glasses, I'm not sure I would have paid attention to the lack of peace, even if I had known the rule.

I continued to have an unsettling feeling in the pit of my stomach as I left the house, so I decided to include God in my decision. After praying, I heard: "*You can, but it is not what is best.*" I grimaced, pondered for a moment, then mentally deleted all but the "*you can*" and forged ahead. As in the lyrics of "*Bringing in the Sheaves*" I went into the office rejoicing and came back rejoicing.

I was more than ready to show off my new eyes and my new outlook toward my frameless future. But my excitement was short-lived. Within days, my contacts irritated my eyes so much it felt as if I were peeling onions. I tried a number of different contact cleaners, but none of them brought relief.

I should have just pitched the lenses in the trash. But since frugality and vanity superseded logic, in spite of my misery, I continued to peel back my eyelids every morning and try again. That is—until I had a dream in which God warned me that I would go blind if I continued to wear my contacts.

The dream was so vivid I was awakened out of a sound sleep. However, since my fear of acceptance was greater than the warning, I decided to dismiss the dream and set about my usual morning routine of putting in my contacts. Usual, however, quickly became the unusual. As I was perched on the bathroom counter top with my finger in my eye, my two-year old son walked in, looked up at me and said in a very stern voice, "Momma, Jesus said NO!"

That did it! E. F. Hutton could have been in the room. As my hand dropped from my eye, my jaw dropped to my chest. After all, when God sends in a two year old to warn you—you'd better listen!

I thought the contact solutions were the only problem, but later on my optometrist informed me that the contacts themselves were irritating my eyes. I learned an important lesson from that little incident, and I kept the contacts (in their boxes, of course) for a couple of years as a reminder. Paul writes in 1 Corinthians 6:12, "Everything is permissible (allowable and lawful) for me; but not all things are helpful (good for me to do, expedient and profitable when considered with other things)" (AMP). Just because something isn't wrong doesn't mean it's good.

There is nothing wrong with contacts in and of themselves. Many people wear them with no problems, but God knew that they were not beneficial for *me*.

Instead of withholding from me, He was trying to protect me and show me a better way.

♥ *Heart Encounter* ♥

1. Can you think of a time in your life when you chose what *seemed good* over what was *best*? What was the result?

2. Unfortunately, I can think of numerous times when God, in His goodness, tried to direct me toward His best when I wouldn't listen. Mistakenly, I believed He was withholding instead of protecting. Have you ever thought that God was withholding from you? If so, why?

3. I can think of some instances when my children have wanted something so badly that they ignored any advice I gave them. On a few occasions I have told them, "Okay, go ahead then." Even though I made my concerns clear to them, I gave them the liberty to choose. Sure enough, they ended up regretting their decisions, even though they learned valuable lessons. Do you believe that there are times when God will

allow you and me to "go ahead anyway" even if He knows it is not what is best for us? Why?

4. I have also discovered, at times, there are things in my life that are not beneficial to me about which I haven't even asked the Holy Spirit's counsel. For example, I used to be unaware that God even cared about what I listened to or watched. Until one night while watching a show on TV, He spoke to my heart, *"I'd rather you not watch that."* Have you ever asked the Lord to reveal His *best* for you concerning your choices of entertainment? Are you willing to ask Him now?

Through lessons like the one I learned with my contact lenses, I have become aware that *you can* doesn't always mean that *you should.* As Christians, you and I are surrounded by a world of *you cans*—things that are not necessarily *unlawful,* but definitely not *helpful* to our spirits, our minds, our bodies, or our lives. The question is: Are we willing to listen to the little and not so little nudges of the Holy Spirit and trust God for His best?

Let's Pray:

Lord, make me sensitive to the nudges of your Spirit. Guard me and guide me in all of my decisions. I don't want my life to be centered around just what is lawful. I want you also to lead me into what is profitable—for me, for others, and for my growth in you. Help me to set my heart on what is *best*, not on just what seems *good* to me. Thank you for being interested in even the minutest details of my life. You know the number of hairs on my head, and you know the plans that you have for me. As in Jeremiah 29:11, I can be confident that just as you have promised, your plans are to bring me peace, and to give me a future and a hope. In Jesus' Name…Amen!

Reflections:

_____

_____

_____

_____

_____

_____

_____

_____

_____

Just Squish It

I hate roaches! They absolutely disgust me! Mom once told me my phobia of roaches could be because of an odor that they emit. While there might be some validity to her comment, I think a few childhood experiences may have also contributed to my aversion.

I grew up in a humid climate where roaches were a continual nuisance. One night, I vividly remember being awakened by my father's deep commanding voice, "Jeannie, don't move!" Looking through partially opened eyelids, I could make out Dad's form standing over me with a fly swatter. "There is a large roach on your forehead," he continued. "Be still so I can kill it!"

Needless to say, not only did I move, I moved so quickly that I probably set a world record. Although my father wasn't too thrilled about my disobedience, he did answer my inquiry as to why the roach was on my forehead by explaining the thing was probably heading toward my mouth in search for water. From then on I developed a habit of sleeping with a sheet over my head.

(Hmmmm---I wonder why?)

I remember another incident as a youngster. I was removing a box from my closet when I felt something squish under my fingers. To my horror, when I retrieved my hand, it was covered with roach guts. Yuck! I freaked out! I must have looked pretty funny walking around with my arm dangling by my side for the next few days. But no matter how many times I washed my hand, in my eyes, it was contaminated and rendered useless until I was thoroughly satisfied that all of the roach cooties were gone. I vowed thereafter to be more cautious when retrieving items from my closet.

Not only did the disgusting little beasts keep me on guard during the day, they began to invade my childhood dreams. There were thousands of them. They had personalities, lived in a kingdom, and pursued with a vengeance anyone who murdered one of their kind. Waking up in the middle of the night with fresh visions of roaches running through my little head, I would force myself to think of roaring oceans and snow-capped mountaintops until the horrid images dissipated. Although this technique did seem to relieve some of my nightmares, it did nothing to calm my fears.

The irony was that no matter how much I despised roaches, I couldn't bring myself to squish them. I had frequently observed my father and siblings annihilate them with shoes, flyswatters, and an assortment of other miscellaneous objects within their grasp. I even saw dad cut one in half with a kitchen knife once. Yuck! That really turned my stomach, but I could not follow suit. This might have been partially due to the fact that no matter the method of extermination, I was always repulsed at the carnage that remained. Why did God give them so many guts anyway? Floors and counters had to be wiped, shoes had to be scraped, and fly swatters had to be rinsed. Yet, even then, something seemed to always be left behind—even if it were just a stray leg or head that showed up a few days later.

Unfortunately, my "roach phobia" continued into my adulthood. I could handle spiders or just about any other creepy crawly critter, but the sight of a roach would send me fleeing from the room until a terminator would come to my aid and issue the "death blow." On occasions when no such person could be found, I was forced to resort to more *creative methods*.

One such instance was in my mid-twenties. I was awakened out of a sound sleep by a peculiar noise. Since the scratching sound seemed magnified by the stillness of the night, I thought that maybe a mouse was in my room. Cautiously sliding out of bed and tip toeing over to the dresser, I proceeded to carefully lift up a few papers. To my horror, I came face to antenna with one of the largest roaches that I had ever seen! Since my husband Joe was at work, I had no Cavalry to call in, so I quickly gathered my bedding, closed the door behind me, and retreated to the living room. After flipping on the kitchen light I settled down on the couch with hopes of resuming my slumber.

As soon as I laid my head down on my pillow, I noticed a wide gap under the bedroom door. I got up and gathered some towels from the bathroom, and spent the next few minutes stuffing them into the opening until I was sure that no passage was available. As an extra precaution, I also rolled up a couple of towels and pushed them against the sides to finish my barricade. "Now," I thought to myself, "That should do it!"

I laid back down and attempted to sleep, but every time I would start to drift off, my eyes would jerk wide open and stare at the little fortress made of towels, wondering if there was any possible way of escape I hadn't calculated. Just when I had convinced myself my plan was "foolproof," I noticed a tiny speck of black. The speck began to grow as my eyes remained riveted to the center of the towels. I was both amazed and repulsed as I watched my jello-bodied captive make its way through the layers of cloth.

"How did it get through?" I questioned.

My prisoner having escaped, it was time to resort to more drastic measures. No more Mrs. Nice Gal! Two-inch Goliath stood before me, and he was going down!!! I wish that I could tell you that I grabbed the nearest shoe and leveled him, but that was not *exactly* the case. Instead, I opted for a less messy method—*the can of death!*

Sliding gently off the couch so as not to startle my foe, I slowly crept into the kitchen, opened the cabinet and retrieved a can of bug spray. I wasn't supposed to use insecticides because of my history of chemical allergies, but I rationalized that my current circumstance called for an exception to the rule.

Now, fully armed and dangerous, I continued my advance toward the object of my disgust. Gently placing my finger on the trigger, I cautiously stalked my victim. When I was within twelve inches of my nemesis, I applied pressure to the spray nozzle and released about a fifteen second blast as I frantically chased the little bugger around the room, all the while locked in on him like a fighter pilot on an enemy target. When I was thoroughly convinced of his imminent demise (seeing him lying on his back kicking his legs in slow motion was a pretty good indication) I retreated back to the couch, gagging and struggling for air. As I fought back the tears from my stinging eyes and felt the burning in my throat, I thought to myself, "That stupid roach might not be the *only* thing that dies tonight!"

My encounter with the roach reminds me a lot of how sin often operates in our lives. Just as my fear of roaches initially led me not to take action, sometimes you and I continue in habitual sin because it seems easier to stay in denial than to face our fears of rejection, loss, pain, and exposure. When we are finally put in a position where we have to *face* our sinful attitudes or choices, although we may be disgusted by them, we might try to either continue to avoid them or go through a crazy series of spiritual or emotional gymnastics in order to barricade them. We may even resort to measures that harm us in order to get rid of them. Instead of trying to deal with our ungodly behaviors in our own strength and understanding, we need to surrender the battle to God, realize that we already have the victory through Christ's sacrifice, and ask for God's wisdom and strength to just *squish* them. There may be a few guts to clean up, especially if others are involved, but, thankfully, it is nothing that God can't handle!

By the way, I do squish roaches with shoes now! I just make sure that they are not *my* shoes!

♥ *Heart Encounter* ♥

1. Sometimes, I have allowed ungodly behaviors to continue in my life because I was afraid of feeling loss—loss of relationship, loss of pleasure, loss of approval, loss of excitement, loss of security, loss of privacy, etc. Can you relate? If so, explain.

2. A few years ago I heard a woman give an inspirational message about trusting God. I was impacted by one of her statements: "If God removes something from your life it is because He has something better to give you." What are some good things that God wants to give you?

3. Read 1 John 1:6-10. We are not always aware of our sinful attitudes and actions. That is why we need the Holy Spirit to shine the light of His presence and illuminate the hidden things that are hindering us. Are you seeking God's presence? Is there something that He is revealing to you?

4. Although the roach in my story was only a couple of inches long, when I confronted it, it seemed *huge*. As you and I are brought face-to-face with our sins, especially *the little sins of our hearts*, they often will seem huge and intimidating. Can you think of a time in your life when God brought you revelation concerning ungodly behaviors or attitudes? Is He doing that now? Explain.

5. We each have a hole in our soul that only God can fill. The more we allow His presence to come in, the more He reveals. His purpose in revealing what is in our hearts is to bring us healing and deepen our relationship with Him. I have noticed when God reveals my sinful behaviors or ungodly thought patterns, the Roaring Lion (the devil) will do everything he can to get me to retreat. When the devil rears his ugly head, I have learned to acknowledge God's unconditional love for me, stand in my identity in Christ, fight with the Word, and enter into the

Lord's presence through worship in order to be victorious. Have you ever noticed the battle increasing right before God gave you a victory? Give an example of the attack and of how you received the victory.

6. I mentioned I don't squish roaches with my own shoes. But when it comes to our ungodly behaviors, our own shoes (knowing our identity in Christ) are the most effective weapons we have. If you and I try to base our growth on the approval of others and/or if we, after receiving salvation, still see ourselves as sinners instead of saints who sins have been paid for by Jesus' blood, shame will keep us from receiving the free gift of grace that has already been given to us (Romans 4). Knowing that we are dearly loved children robed in the righteousness of Christ will cause us to desire God's presence and freedom from whatever is holding us back from His best. Do you see yourself as a sinner or as a precious child of God whose sins are already covered by the blood of Jesus?

In Matthew 5:29-30 Jesus gives the following instruction: "If your right eye causes you to sin, pluck it out and cast *it* from you; for it is more profitable for you that one of your members perish, than for your whole body to be cast into hell. And if your right hand causes you to sin, cut it off and cast *it* from you; for it is more profitable for you that one of your members perish, than for your whole body to be cast into hell." In these scriptures, Jesus is not promoting self-mutilation or dismemberment. He is telling us to cut off the things in our lives that are hindering us because He loves us and wants what is best for us. Are you ready to ask God to reveal and heal ungodly beliefs or choices in your life, believing that you will receive His grace, wisdom, and strength to *squish* the things that are hindering you from moving forward?

Let's Pray:

Precious Lord, thank you for always loving me. Expose the sinful behaviors and thought patterns in my life so I can be free. As you bring those things which may have been hidden to the forefront, let me not retreat. Give me the wisdom and courage to stand fast in my identity in you and *squish* my sins instead of avoiding them or trying to kill them by my own means. I am thankful that you have given me authority over the enemy through the blood of Jesus Christ, and that the victory is mine. I also trust you to fill the empty places in my soul and to clean up the guts resulting from my sinful choices; including how they have affected the lives of those around me. Turn all my *messes* into *messages*! Thank you for your love and faithfulness in the process. In Jesus' Name…Amen!

Reflections:

_____
_____
_____
_____
_____
_____
_____

Betrayed

I sat on the edge of my bed, hot tears streaming down my face, my body quivering, my heart pounding—growing in intensity with each subsequent beat until I feared that it might burst from my chest. My tormented body mirrored my tormented mind.

"How could he do this to me?"

As my dreams of our future life together lay shattered, all the years of prayer, perseverance, and choosing to love a man who was incapable of loving me back, now seemed in vain.

Once more, my eyes darted back and forth across the carefully penned letters on the page. I winced as each stroke screamed of the painstaking effort that had fashioned it. I never knew that Joe was capable of writing so neatly, so delicately.

At first, I tried to convince myself that my husband didn't write the letter. "Maybe he was keeping it for someone else," or "Maybe it was a misunderstanding or some cruel joke." But the stinging reality hit home when

I called Joe and he confirmed my worst fears. I had been betrayed!

The last forty-eight hours had been a waking nightmare. No matter how hard I tried, I hadn't been able to silence the continuous stream of words from the letter written to another woman that ran like a ticker tape through my mind. Tender words. Romantic words. Words I had longed to hear for 15 years. Words that never interrupted the silence of our marriage, now continuously interrupted the silence of my life, robbing me of both peace and sleep.

The turmoil within me had now reached the boiling point. I not only felt betrayed by my husband, but by God Himself. After all, hadn't I trusted? Hadn't I persevered? When all seemed lost, hadn't I held on believing for that which I *did not see*?! "God! Why? Why did you allow me to believe a lie?" I challenged. "Why did you turn my heart so I could love my enemy? If Joe had chosen to leave years before, when I desperately wanted to be free, it would have been easy. Why now? Why did you take him now? Now, when I *love* him—I feel as if I am being ripped in two."

I'm not sure how long I ranted and raved as I shook the fist of my soul toward Heaven, but at some point I grabbed my pen and journal and begin to pour out in writing all that was churning in my restless being. Frustration, hatred, pain, hopelessness, and betrayal began to spill out beneath my pen into a modern psalm. In the midst of scrawling out my disappointments and animosity to the King of Heaven, the Holy Spirit interrupted my little tirade and took hold of both my pen and my heart. The words that now began to fill the page were not my words. They were words of comfort and understanding from the one Person who truly could relate, and His compassion brought conviction to my spirit and began to sooth my weary soul. *"My child, I know how you feel. I know what it feels like to be betrayed."*

At first, the realization startled me. But then clarity came. Of course, Jesus understood betrayal! He was betrayed by Judas and the rest of the disciples. His closest friends, the men whom He had shared his life with for three years, couldn't tarry with Him one hour in the garden, and then denied and abandoned Him.

In that moment I didn't feel so alone anymore—someone understood—totally understood. Not only did Jesus understand because He had been betrayed, but He also understood because He is the only one who knew me—I mean, who *really* knew me. He knew everything about me. He knew my heart. He knew my pain. He knew every detail of my circumstances—even the unspoken ones. As His peace enveloped me, I pictured myself wrapped in my Heavenly Father's arms and was finally able to go to sleep.

The next part of the revelation came almost a year later while I was observing an Easter pageant our church was putting on for the community. After being thoroughly entertained by the talented voices and beautiful pageantry, my attention was drawn to the small band of actors to the left of the stage. They were ecstatically waving palm fronds, hailing Jesus as King, and welcoming Him into Jerusalem, when abruptly the music and mood changed dramatically. The scene of the trial now played out before my eyes. To my horror, the very same people who had been joyfully celebrating Jesus with palm fronds just minutes before were now shaking their fists and crying out for Christ's crucifixion. I felt a thud in my heart as I saw myself among the crowd.

How many times had I waved palm fronds when I liked a certain outcome, and then turned around and shook my fist when my prayers seemed unanswered or life didn't turn out the way *I* had planned? I thought back to the time when my husband had betrayed me, and during the subsequent divorce. God had been so loving and faithful to me, even when I was shaking my fist and ranting and raving at Him. I knew what it was like to be betrayed. But so did the Lord—not only by Judas and the disciples, but also by me. I had betrayed Him by my lack of trust and my accusing heart, but just as He did on Calvary, instead of condemning me, He opened His arms wide, and extended His forgiveness and grace.

Just as the people in Jerusalem were blinded to the *big picture* (Jesus was not going to reign as an earthly king at that time, but He had come to set them free for all time), I had missed the *big picture* as well. As in Jeremiah 29:11, God knew the plans that He had for me;

they were to prosper me and to give me a future and a hope. He didn't *take* my husband as I had accused; He had merely allowed him to choose his own way—bringing my children and me to a greater freedom. That afternoon, my heart broke, and I repented as I realized I had perceived God's deliverance as betrayal, and my betrayal as justification.

♥ *Heart Encounter* ♥

1. Have you ever been betrayed? Maybe it wasn't your spouse. Maybe instead it was another family member, a co-worker, or a close friend? What was your situation?

2. Have you ever felt betrayed by God when things didn't go as you had planned? Maybe someone else got the promotion, your marriage didn't work, or the loved one that you prayed for didn't live?

3. How do you respond when life just doesn't seem to make sense?

4. There is a popular song called *Blessed Be the Name* which reminds us that Jesus' name is to be blessed at all times, in the good and in the bad. Ecclesiastes 3 tells us that there is a time for everything. What does this scripture speak to you about your current circumstances?

5. While it is true that our circumstances can and will change, what will always remain constant?

6. God is referred to as the Father of Lights in James 1:17 "...with whom there is no variation or shadow of turning." Does it comfort you to know that although your circumstances may change, God always remains the same? How?

7. Read about Joseph in Genesis chapter 37 & 39. On more than one occasion, Joseph was betrayed by those closest to him. It amazes me that he didn't blame God. Unfortunately, I don't think Joseph and I share the same genes. What can we learn from Joseph's example?

Although Joseph was falsely accused and imprisoned he continued to trust God and was faithful. When we are betrayed we can choose to trust God or stay in our prisons of pain. In the midst of heartache and uncertainty we are being fashioned for our destinies. As God grows us and prepares us for the "good plans' He has for us we can receive comfort in knowing that Jesus knows our circumstances, the depth of our emotions, and the final outcomes. For what we may now be blinded to—God sees in full view.

Let's Pray:

Precious Lord, although others may betray me, you are always there for me, desiring what is best for my life. I choose to forgive those who have betrayed me, and I ask forgiveness for the times I have betrayed you in thought as well as in action. I know that you have compassion, and that you completely understand my heart as well as my circumstances. Since you are omniscient, you can see what I do not see. I place my trust in you, knowing that you know the beginning from the end. Thank you for bringing forth your glory out of the hurtful situations in my life. You are always faithful to bring me comfort and peace in the midst of my pain and turmoil. I love you Jesus! Thank you for always loving me! In Jesus' Name...Amen!

Reflections:

_____

_____

_____

_____

_____

_____

_____

_____

The Word Impossible

One of the challenges I had being a single mother was trying to meet the same financial responsibilities on a fourth of the income. Even with cleaning houses, baby sitting, and doing other odd jobs, I was barely paying my bills. Consequently, many of my family and friends thought my decision to continue home schooling, instead of returning to the workforce, was absurd. Every time I would look at the impossibility of my situation, I can't say that I blamed them.

Early one morning, a vision of the word **IMPOSSIBLE** flashed before me like a neon sign. I heard the Lord speak to my heart: *"Take off the I M and add an apostrophe."* In my mind I saw (I'M). Then He told me *"With the I AM all things are POSSIBLE!"* The next two days I woke up with Ezekiel 12:9 going through my head. Although I looked it up on both occasions, the verse didn't make sense. "Son of man, has not the house of Israel, the rebellious house, said to you, 'What are you doing?'"

By the third morning I had the passage memorized, but I still didn't understand its meaning. The Lord then brought me revelation concerning my ex-husband and others: *"Jeannie, Joe is watching you. There are many people watching you, because they do not believe I will take care of you and the children. But I will show my glory in how I provide for you!"*

Years before, I had read a book called *God's Smuggler* by Brother Andrew, the evangelist who founded Open Doors ministry. I decided to read it to the kids. The chapter about the "King's Highway" describes Brother Andrew's financial faith walk. Like George Mueller, an Englishman who was led to trust God to provide for building and maintaining orphanages in Bristol, Brother Andrew was rarely led to share his needs. Instead, he was only to tell them to the Lord and trust that they would be met. It was now time for us to do the same.

When I closed out my bank account a few days later I was amazed to discover there was $2,700 dollars in it. I rejoiced in the unexpected provision. That night, God gave me a dream about trusting Him. When I awoke, I heard, *"Give $2,000 dollars to Celeste."* Celeste was a young woman in our church who was preparing to go on a mission trip to South America. My immediate response was "I rebuke you, Satan, in the name of Jesus! God would not have me take the food from the mouths of my children!"

In my spirit I heard the Lord's tender voice:

"Jeannie, you have got to trust me. You will not be able to care for your children and do what I have for you to do unless you trust me. "I want you to give 20% of everything that comes to you and 50% of everything you earn by your own hand."

As my understanding changed from "This is not God!" to "Oh no! This is God!" I methodically gathered the money I had stashed in my closet, put it in an envelope, and drove to my church. Once I handed it to the secretary I was flooded with peace.

As the children and I stepped out in obedience and gave, supernatural provision began pouring in. I could literally write an entire book (we kept a daily journal we called a *Blessing Book*) just on how the Lord met us in our "faith walk."

When I would pay another single mom's bill or give money to a stranger in the store, sometimes that very day, God would bring others, including sometimes strangers, to give us money or pay our bills. Rarely was it the same person twice and rarely were the encounters similar.

Once at midnight, I was praying for the rest of my house payment. A few minutes later a woman called to tell me that God woke her up and instructed her to send me the $500 she was getting ready to put against the principle on her auto loan. I needed exactly $500.

On another occasion, God provided what He had promised me through a gentleman sitting next to me in an airplane before I arrived at my destination.

But it was the card from an agnostic woman which

contained the $200 that was the answer to our prayer for pellets for our pellet stove that amazed me the most. The card read, "Someone up there is watching out for you. When I stepped into my shower I heard, 'Send Jeannie $200.'"

Each time God met our needs, and even our desires, He continuously revealed to us and to all who were observing our situation that not only is He faithful, but also very creative and quite remarkable.

As I mentioned earlier, I could write an entire book just on the financial miracles, but for now for the sake of time and space I will only share two:

I'll never forget the day when the Lord told me to open the chest freezer and say, "In the name of Jesus be filled!" I wish I could say "Praise God!" was my immediate response. But it was more like, "I'm really losing it this time!" As I walked into the next room, while claiming a sound mind, I heard again, *"Go to the freezer, open it, and say in the name of Jesus be filled."*

"I'm not going to do it! Lord, this time you have gone too far!" was my "oh-ye-of little-faith" response. To which the Lord replied, *"Yes, you will, and you will take Joshua with you when you do!"*

When I told my oldest son Joshua that we were supposed to open the freezer and declare it be filled, he readily jumped to his feet and piped up, "Okay, Mom, let's go for it!" A few minutes later Joshua and I stood in front of the empty chest freezer, lifted the lid, and counted to three. Then we declared with full authority,

"In the name of Jesus be filled!"

I'm not sure what I was expecting when we closed the freezer. Was food going to miraculously appear out of nowhere? I don't even remember if I tried to take a peek before I left for my house-cleaning job. Knowing me, I probably did. What I *do* remember is that I was still worried about our depleted groceries when I went to work. While I was cleaning, the woman I was cleaning for began asking me questions. When she asked if we had enough food, I started getting a little emotional. She explained that she was going on a diet and wanted to get rid of everything she couldn't eat so she wouldn't be tempted.

I followed her to the garage where she opened a large freezer and began to place the contents into boxes. In the midst of my excitement, I held back tears as her husband and I loaded the car with a variety of frozen meat and vegetable entrées, as well as an assortment of desserts. Every time I thought she was through, she filled my arms with more packages.

When I arrived home, the kids jumped up and down and squealed with excitement as they unloaded the bounty and deposited it into the freezer. Not only was there an abundance, there were many expensive items we would never have purchased ourselves. After the chest freezer was full, we still had additional items to put in the kitchen refrigerator's freezer compartment.

I am a firm believer that God initiated the "pay it forward" system long before the movie came out. As I mentioned earlier, the kids and I were led to give twenty percent of everything we received. Ten percent went to the church, but the other ten went to *wherever God said*. It actually became somewhat of a game. Sometimes it went to ministries, sometimes to friends, and sometimes to strangers. Since we gave before paying our bills or buying groceries, it was not uncommon for us to give away hundred dollar bills. When distributing the money, we usually were met with disbelief, followed by "How can I accept this?" This was especially true in cases where the person knew us. However, not only were *we* blessed to be a blessing, we often saw those who gave to us receive blessings in return.

The kids and I were taking the "King's Highway" seriously. King's kids don't beg; they ask believing that if it is the will of God, they will receive. That is why when we prayed about taking in a troubled teen, we asked not just for provision, but for God's best. Since it was unanimously decided that bunk beds were a necessity, although we were used to hand-me-down everything, we stepped out and asked the Lord for brand new beds, mattresses, and bedding. Within a week, my friend Betty called and asked if she and her husband Martin could come over. I had been meeting and praying with Betty and a couple of other women who were in abusive relationships. Since Martin had threatened the family and left, I had advised Betty to do whatever it took to keep her and her children safe. So when she informed me that Martin had had an incredible encounter with the Lord and had repented, I was leery. However, she insisted and told me, "Jeannie, Martin said he's supposed to talk to you." At that point, I prayed and God told me to meet with them.

Upon their arrival, I immediately noticed Martin's entire demeanor was different. He was obviously filled with humility as he shared one of the most incredible testimonies of conversion and transformation I had ever heard. As we all held hands and prayed, the presence of the Lord was so sweet none of us wanted to end our meeting, but Martin had to run and get their son from school.

Over the next hour (although Betty and I continued to talk and share our amazement about all that the Lord had done), every twenty minutes or so, she would quizzically insert, "Hmm, I wonder what is taking Martin so long?" When he did eventually return with their son in tow, Martin was behaving strangely. His skin was pale and he was trembling. He kept repeating, "I've never done anything like this before."

His wife and I were both puzzled and concerned, until he related all that had transpired after he left the house. On his way to pick up their son he heard God loudly speak to him (that alone had never happened to him before). He said that he was instructed to go to the bank and take out five hundred dollars and give it to Jeannie. As he held out the money, he reiterated, "Nothing like this has ever happened to me before!"

At first I hesitated to accept the gift, but then the

Holy Spirit reminded me of our prayer for beds and bedding. When I shared about the children and my prayers, the couple was overjoyed with the confirmation, and we praised and prayed again before they left.

A few days later I got a call from Betty. She was brimming with excitement. She said when Martin gave me the money they were not even aware of how much was in their account. As it ended up, they would have been short on their bills. The following day they went to a family reunion, and one of their relatives walked up to Martin and gave him a check—for no apparent reason. The check was for $1,000. God had already doubled what they had given!

Once again, God had brought forth the double portion and accomplished the impossible; not only in the restoration of this couple's marriage, but in the reinstating of their faith, which impacted many lives as they ministered to others through their amazing testimony. And once again, I could hear my mother's words, "You can't out love or out give God."

♥ *Heart Encounter* ♥

1. Although, I have seen the Lord provide in so many incredible ways, there are still times when I begin to doubt. Instead of "Wow Lord! How are you going to do it this time?" I can easily fall back into "Are you

going to do it this time?" It all boils down to trust. Do you ever find yourself struggling with trusting God's provision or plan for you? Why do you think this is so?

2. Read 1 Kings 17:8-16. Do you think it was by accident that Elijah was sent to a poor widow to ask for provision? Why do you think God chose her instead of someone who had plenty?

3. During our "faith walk," I sometimes had difficulty receiving blessings from certain people. Once, when I was praying and inquiring why God was leading a certain person to do so much, He responded, *"Because he is the one who needs the blessing."* Do you think that Elijah was sent to receive from the poor widow because she was the one who *needed* the blessing?

4. What if the widow had refused? What if she had been so wrapped up in her own survival that she refused to give the little she had? Just think of what she would have missed—not only the provision of her sustenance but also the resurrection of her son (1 Kings 17:17-24).

5. Many times, I have been led to give my last, only to see it multiplied back to me. But there are other times when I have held on tightly, afraid to let go. Whenever I start thinking that *I* need to be in control, I find myself struggling with trust. When I let go of what I have, peace and blessings are released in my life. Can you think of a time in your life when peace and blessings were released when you chose to let go? What did it look like?

6. The widow with the son not only had to let go of the last of what she had for herself, she also had to let go of what she had for her son. Sometimes when God has us step out in faith, the enemy will try to convince us that not only are we terrible stewards, but also that we are terrible parents. Keep in mind, just as in the case of the widow and her son, God is faithful. Do you believe that God knows your family's circumstances and that He is perfectly capable of meeting *all* your needs?

No matter what your situation, God is in control. He is faithful to provide both needs and opportunities for growth. Faith and trust are not passive. Instead of the widow being blessed with an abundance of bags of grain, she had to take action and exercise faith everyday as she scooped out the flour and mixed in the oil. I wonder how many times she looked down in the containers in utter amazement, realizing that she had her supply for the next meal.

Sometimes God will bring in truckloads of blessings, but often He will supply just enough to keep us believing for more. Sometimes that *more* will be our daily needs, sometimes it will include the needs of friends and family as well, and sometimes God will enlarge our vision so much, it will even include the needs of the world. Yes, God is truly the great **I AM** and with the **I AM** all things are possible!

Let's Pray:

Dear Lord, I am so thankful that nothing is impossible for you. Help me to be faithful when you call me to give, knowing that not only does giving open up blessings for my family, but stepping out in faith teaches me to trust you more. In allowing myself to be a vessel of provision to others, I get to be a part of the exciting things you are doing in hearts and lives, whether they are in the lives around me that I can see or in lives of others around the world. Multiply everything that comes into my hands, and bless me to be a blessing as you have me seed into what is dear to your heart. In Jesus' Name...Amen!

Reflections:

_____

_____

_____

_____

_____

_____

_____

_____

A Walk in the Desert

I had been faithfully giving and I mean literally (by faith) for about seven months, when I began losing my joy in my *faith journey*. The same challenges that previously would have stirred thankfulness in my heart now brought forth grumbling and complaining. Statements like, "God, how much longer?" and "At least when I was married I didn't have to worry about the house payment," often rumbled around in my mind as I lamented not being self-supportive.

One afternoon, in the midst of one of my pity parties, I grabbed my last fifty dollars and a couple of my children and went grocery shopping. After filling the cart with about forty-eight dollars worth of necessities and gliding it into the checkout lane—No.3, to be exact—I happened to glance back and see a woman I knew a few aisles away. I heard in my spirit: *"Give her your fifty dollars."*

I freaked out. "I can't do that!" I argued. "How am I supposed to pay for my groceries?"

"Write a check," God replied.

After inwardly fussing and fuming about how it could not possibly be God's will for me to write a "hot check," I tossed the remaining few items on the counter, instructed my daughter, "Wait right here!" and I *went about my Father's business.* Doesn't that last phrase sound noble? In reality, I literally stomped over to where the dear woman was stationed with her cart, jerked out my hand, and barked, "Here, God told me to give you this!" Startled, she replied, "Oh Jeannie, I can't take this from you. You can't afford it."

I wish I could say I leapt through the open door provided by her last statement and began to share God's goodness in my life and instances of His supernatural provision. But instead, I snapped back, "Just take it!" After I had thrust the money into her hand, I walked back to the register and grudgingly wrote out a check, all the while murmuring that it was sure to bounce. Then I gathered my groceries and my children, and left in a huff.

I grumbled and complained to God all of the way to the car: "It's just too hard! You ask too much! Haven't I done everything you have asked me to do? I've already given my twenty percent and now you want *more!*"

As I stood next to my car, the Holy Spirit stopped me in mid-rant and illuminated the ugliness in my heart. Tears began streaming down my face, and I sobbed the entire drive home. I was so distraught when I pulled into the driveway that instead of unloading the car, I ran to my room, dropped to my knees and began to wail, "Oh

God, deliver me! Change my heart! Help me to be thankful! I don't want to be an Old Testament Israelite! I don't want to be an Israelite! I don't want to be an Israelite!"

I curled up on the floor with my hands over my face, feeling like an outcast, awaiting God's wrath. But instead of condemnation, the Lord began to comfort me, affirm me, and surround me with His peace. Praise began to flow from my lips. It was now time to leave the desert of grumbling and cross the Jordan River to thankfulness.

After I rose from my bedroom floor—and my ungratefulness—I felt led to call my bank. Unbeknownst to me, there was a hundred dollars in my account. Once again, the Lord proved that He goes before and prepares the way.

Because of The Lord's confirmation and peace I was able to stay thankful throughout the rest of the week, even when my child support check didn't arrive. In spite of the shortage, the kids and I again witnessed God accomplish the impossible by gifting us with anonymous groceries and money. So much was His faithfulness that I only needed to purchase twenty dollars worth of items when I went shopping the following week.

As I was handing the cashier my $20, a boy of about thirteen, who looked vaguely familiar, came up to me and said, "My Mother told me to give this to you from Jesus." He then handed me a fifty-dollar bill; immediately, my eyes began to water.

Since I recognized the boy's mother from a church

we had attended quite a few years before, I graciously accepted the money, paid for my purchases, and met her over by the door. "Jeannie, I hope you don't mind," she said. "Sometimes God tells us to give money to people, and He told me to give you fifty dollars." I started to laugh. Then I shared the story of how during the previous week, God had mercifully met me in the midst of my grumbling and exposed the ungratefulness in my desert-dwelling heart.

After my old acquaintance and I had briefly caught up on what had transpired in our families during the past few years, my daughter Shanna piped up, "Mom, do you realize this is the same time of the day and the same day of the week when you were led to give away that fifty dollar bill?" Her statement made me stop in my tracks. "What are the odds?" I thought to myself. But the wonder of it all stepped up yet another notch before we walked outside, as my daughter with a sense of awe, once again interjected, "Mom, we checked out in lane three that time too!" Same lane—same time of the day—same day of the week—different heart. Thank you Jesus!

Once again, the Lord was proving to us that He is into multiplication, for it was amazing how He multiplied that original fifty dollars. Over the next few months I often ran into the woman who had blessed me with the fifty dollars at the grocery store. During our second chance meeting, which was just weeks after the initial one, we were both amazed that we had met up twice in such a short while after not having seen each other for so many years. She again was led to give me some money. She said that the Lord told her that she was supposed to give me money every time she saw me.

I didn't count how many times that was, but over the next few months the situation almost became comical. I began to feel so guilty I almost dreaded going shopping for fear that I might run into her, causing her to part with more. I doubt if she ever felt that way, but I could only think of how *I* might have felt in the same situation. I could just see her pulling into the parking lot, slumped down behind the wheel of her car cautiously glancing back and forth, perusing the lines of stationary vehicles to see if *mine* was among them. If my car wasn't in site, I imagined her exiting her van, running into the store, hurriedly buying what she needed, and making a mad dash back toward the parking lot to retreat to the safety of her home.

Of course, she and her family were not like that at all. As a matter of fact, the last time we ran into them, we were Christmas shopping with Christmas money they had mailed us! How God blessed us through their family during that season and how He multiplied a mere fifty dollars into over four hundred dollars still amazes me. After that Christmas, God miraculously shut that door of provision just as quickly as He had opened it, and it was years before we ran into each other again.

♥ *Heart Encounter* ♥

1. In the above story, I have given an example about when I was definitely not practicing thankfulness. Can you think of times in your life where you have grumbled to God? Give an example.

2. Throughout the book of Exodus, the children of Israel continually grumbled and complained. Unfortunately, I can relate to them more than I would like to admit. In examining my own heart and life, I believe that complaining is an outward manifestation of a heart full of self and mistrust. What do you think?

3. I used to judge the Old Testament Israelites. I thought, "Surely, I wouldn't have a problem with trust if I saw the Red Sea parted and quail fall from the sky!" But even after witnessing God's miraculous provision in other ways for so many years, I sometimes still catch myself complaining and doubting the Lord's provision. Can you relate?

4. A friend once shared with me that she felt God never blessed her. As she began to lament about witnessing so many miracles in my life without receiving any of

her own, I encouraged her to start a blessing book. I then reminded her of the provision I had observed concerning her and her children, including a time when I was led to give her money. She had simply forgotten. Have you ever *forgotten* what God has done for you? Why do you think that is?

5. When you and I are discouraged, the enemy will try to keep us from remembering God's faithfulness. Can you recall testimonies when God met you in difficult times? If you are having trouble remembering, pray and ask God to call to mind times when He provided. You may want to also ask a friend or family member to help you.

6. In Joshua chapter four, the Israelites were led to set up stones of remembrance after they crossed the Jordan into Canaan. Verses 21 and 22 tell us that Joshua spoke to the children of Israel, saying: "When your children ask their fathers in time to come, saying, 'What *are* these stones?' Then you shall let your children know, saying, 'Israel crossed over this Jordan on dry land.'" This is one of the reasons why I encourage people to write down their testimonies. Our testimonies are the stones of remembrance for the coming generations that bear witness to God's faithfulness. Are you setting up your stones?

As I mentioned earlier, the kids and I kept a blessing book during our *faith walk*. Some entries are simply thank-yous to the Lord listing the food and other items He provided that day. Other entries are more detailed, like the story of the fifty dollars. There are also a couple of times when life seemed so difficult the only thing entered was "Thank you for my breath." The goal of the book was not just to set up the stones of remembrance, but also to train our hearts to be thankful.

I thought of the Israelites another time when I had made my children cookies, and my labor of love was met with nothing but complaints. I wondered how God must feel when we whine and complain. Although He does so much for us, we are often ungrateful. I began to wonder if things would have been different for the Old Testament desert dwellers had they had thankful hearts when they encountered obstacles like water problems, lack of food, and giants, instead of accusing the Lord of depriving them and trying to annihilate them. Would they just have had manna and quail or might there have been provision of some fruits and veggies as well? I guess we will never know.

Let's Pray:

Dear Lord, help me to have a thankful heart that blesses you. I choose to trust you in all circumstances, knowing you love me and you know what is best. Since the way I view and spend the money you entrust to me directly correlates to what is in my heart, I realize that you will test me and stretch me in this area. Help me to be obedient as you call me to step out in faith. May I give cheerfully—not fearing lack, but expecting the incredible things you are going to do next. I love you, Lord! In Jesus' Name...Amen!

Reflections:

_____

_____

_____

_____

_____

_____

_____

_____

Obey Without Delay

I once heard a man say that he believed that God's blessings are not contingent on obedience. Although I agree that God is a good father who continually pours blessings upon us, whether we are aware of them or not, I have also learned that sometimes disobedience *does* have a cost.

One such scenario began when my sister-in-law showed up wearing the dress of my dreams to her husband's graduation from the police academy. It was both eloquent and delicate with an empire waistline that was set off by exquisite embroidered lace edging with a contrasting black and white crepe bodice and skirt. With every step she took, the swish of the fabric seemed to scream my name. I thought about buying a dress like it, but when I learned it cost $50, I decided to sew one instead. When I arrived home I went to a fabric store to buy the necessary items, but the cost of just the fabric and the lace alone exceeded my budget, so I had to let it go. "If God wants me to have a similar dress," I reasoned, "He can lead me to one on clearance."

About a month later, I caught site of a yard sale sign as I was running a few quick errands before lunch. Although I immediately felt to turn around because there was a blessing for me at the sale, I kept going, asking the Lord to hold whatever He had for me until I returned. When I arrived at the sale about twenty minutes later, I snagged a shimmery, pretty green dress for $2 off the clothesline and rejoiced in my heart for the wonderful blessing. However, when I approached the cash box table to pay for it, to my horror, I noticed the black and white crepe dress the woman in front of me was purchasing. Not only was it identical to my sister-in law's dress, it was brand new. And it was my size! I thought I was going to die as I read the scribbled price of $3 next to the original $49 price tag dangling by the sleeve. I internally lamented, "God, why didn't you hold it for me as I had requested?"

As I drove home with the green dress that had suddenly lost its luster in the seat next to me, the Lord let me know that I had missed a blessing. DUH! My hesitating instead of instantly obeying had resulted in me losing what had been set apart for me. It was then the Holy Spirit impressed upon my heart that although *this* time my delayed obedience cost me a dress, in the future, my delayed obedience could cost me much more. I realized, right then and there, that would be a lesson that I would not want to learn.

❤ *Heart Encounter* ❤

1. Deuteronomy 11:27 reiterates that blessings come as a result of obedience. Can you think of a time when you paid a price because of disobedience? If so, what was the situation?

2. My pastor has said on many occasions that delayed obedience is disobedience. Do you agree or disagree? Why or why not?

3. There are many instances of immediate obedience in the scriptures: the calling of Simon and Andrew is just one of them. When Jesus called the disciples, they immediately followed Him. Do you believe that we should hesitate when we know it's time to follow?

4. In my experience with the dress, I felt an urgency to go to the sale. At what point do you think I was in disobedience? Explain your answer.

5. Looking back, I believe that as soon as I felt led to turn around but chose for my own convenience to continue to keep going, I had moved into

disobedience. My bargaining with God to hold whatever He had for me was just an attempt to rationalize my choice to disobey while hoping for my desired outcome. Can you think of times when you have tried to strike a bargain with God in order to rationalize disobedience?

6. In the Old Testament, the Israelites were given promises if they would obey the Lord and walk in His ways. Read Deuteronomy chapter 30. What were some of the promises recorded?

7. Do you believe that your obedience today can have the same results in your life as the promises in Deuteronomy? Why or why not?

8. In Deuteronomy chapter 30:14&15 God tells the Israelites through Moses: "See, I set before you today life and prosperity, death and destruction. For I command you today to love the LORD your God, to walk in obedience to him, and to keep his commands, decrees and laws; then you will live and increase, and the LORD your God will bless you in the land you are entering to possess." In reading this passage do you believe that God's intentions are to punish or to protect and prosper?

God's ways bring life. Obeying the Lord means choosing to trust Him—trust Him with our hearts, our plans—our lives. When we obey Him and come into agreement with His heart for us we make covenant with His plans and purposes for us. Since God disciplines or redirects those He loves, I believe it was God's love that allowed me to suffer the consequences of my delayed obedience. Something as simple as a dress doesn't seem like much. But the Lord knew that the loss of a dress that (1) I really wanted, (2) believed it impossible to have; (3) was found two states away; (4) was exactly my size; (5) and was priced at such a great bargain, would open up my understanding to a much bigger picture—for what may seem trivial today may very well save a life tomorrow.

Let's Pray:

Lord, teach me to obey quickly and completely. Thank you for your loving discipline when I do not. I know that you have my best interests in mind. Just as a caring father would expect his children to obey him quickly—for he knows that delayed obedience could cause them to miss blessings or put them in harm's way—you desire me to obey without delay. Thank you for the blessings of provision and protection. I love you! In Jesus' Name...Amen!

Reflections:

_____

_____

_____

_____

_____

_____

_____

_____

_____

Fast

"Fast until the baby comes."

I know that sounds crazy, but that is exactly what God told me to do before the birth of our fourth and last child. When I'd gone in for my checkup earlier that morning, my obstetrician tried to convince me to go to the hospital and have the baby right away. "You're already 6½ centimeters dilated, 100 percent effaced, and the baby is engaged," he reported. "Besides, I'm leaving to go hunting this afternoon."

"But I'm *not* in labor," I responded.

My obstetrician then told me that he could remedy that by inducing my labor with Potossin, a medication that sets up contractions.

"Uh, no thank you!" I replied. I had already had one delivery with Potossin that resulted in my contractions being more severe and closer together. So if at all possible, I was going to avoid another, especially since I had my first three babies without any pain medication.

As I waddled out of the doctor's office, I clearly

heard, *"Fast until the baby comes!"*

"Alright, God," I consented. Since it felt as if the baby was going to fall out any minute anyway, I figured I could handle skipping a meal or two.

That was Thursday! By Saturday morning I was frustrated and ready to throw a little temper tantrum. For the past couple of days, I had been setting leftovers aside for when I could "eat" again. In the meantime, what had seemed like a small request to fast had become a huge challenge. As I lay in bed envisioning the contents of the containers I had stored in my refrigerator, I began to fuss, "Fast? I *have* been fasting and *still* no baby! I'm hungry! Neither the baby nor I can afford to lose weight. Nobody fasts before they have a baby. It's ridiculous!"

After I finished my little spiel, God reminded me that He could do *all* things, even if that meant gaining weight without eating. Then He told me, *"Fast until the baby comes. Your life depends on it!"*

A short time later, I started having contractions and within a few hours I had delivered our beautiful son. My husband Joe and I had agreed if the baby was our prophesied Caleb Daniel (that's another story) I would get my tubes tied. So when the record showed I hadn't eaten in over 48 hours, I was immediately taken into surgery. Before I left the room I made Joe promise that he would bring me a hamburger, French fries, and a chocolate shake so I could gorge once I got out of recovery.

I awoke over four hours later, groggy and in

incredible pain. Through blurred vision I could see Joe and my doctor standing at the foot of my bed. Joe was holding a fast food bag. Even though I felt terrible, as soon as I saw the shake in Joe's hand I began to salivate. That is when I noticed the doc shaking his head. The doctor then said, "I have good news and bad news. Which do you want first?" Before I could answer he began, "You were in surgery for over 3 hours. When I did your tubal you had two hernias. I caught the first one, but since I didn't see the second, I ended up cutting into your intestines. So you have had an intestinal repair as well."

"So what's the good news?" I muttered. The doc perked up a bit. "The good news is since you didn't have any food in your system, there was no leakage so you haven't been poisoned." Then as a plus he added, "I'm also not going to charge you for the hernia or intestinal surgeries."

"Oh! There is *one* more bit of bad news. You are not going to be able to eat anything until tomorrow." Hungry, and disappointed, I mentally rehearsed my surgeries: one tubal, two hernia repairs, and one intestinal repair—but **NO** poisoning! "Thank you, Lord, for having me fast!"

♥ *Heart Encounter* ♥

1. As I was recovering from my surgeries I remember being in awe that God had already known what was going to happen in the operating room. Although I'd been growing in my understanding of His individual *knowledge* of me, the thought of His going *before me* in order to *protect* me, heightened my understanding of His *care* for me. Does it encourage you to know that God goes *before you*?

2. A great example of God *going before* is found in the book of Joshua. The sixth chapter of Joshua begins with God promising Joshua that He had "delivered" (past tense) Jericho into Joshua's hands. But then God tells Joshua that he needs to march with his armed men around the city for six days. Then on the seventh, march seven times and have the priests blow the trumpets. God miraculously collapsed the walls, but Joshua had to follow instructions. God knew about my hernias and He went before, but I needed to follow instructions and *fast* in order to see the victory. Can you think of a time when God *went before* and gave you a victory? Was there anything you were supposed to do in order to receive your victory?

3. Although I didn't realize it at the time, my fasting before Caleb's birth was for physical reasons. The majority of the time, when I am led to fast for others as well as for myself, I have some understanding. But at other times, I do not. All I know is that fasting brings results. Although I can't explain *how* it works, I can tell you I have seen incredible answers to prayer and gained much insight when I have fasted. Have you ever fasted? If so, what have been the results of your fasting?

4. Whether fasting is about bearing another's burdens, intimacy with God, gaining personal understanding, healing, or experiencing spiritual breakthrough, this simple act of denying the flesh moves the heavenlies. One of the scriptures that reminds me of the importance of fasting is found in Matthew 17:21. When Jesus explains to the disciples why they could not cast the demon out of the boy, he addresses their lack of faith and then says, "However, this kind does not go out except by prayer and fasting." Is there a situation about which God is calling you to fast?

Due to my history of drug sensitivities, I had refused all pain meds after my surgery—for fear that they might negatively affect my son. So when a little nurse came in my room at two in the morning, I was in excruciating pain, not just from the surgeries, but also from the after birth contractions. After she emphatically told me, "No one goes without pain meds after a major surgery!" I agreed to take an over-the-counter medicine with Codeine in it. That is when she asked me, "Why did you fast?" When I told her I fasted because God told me to, her face softened and with an almost wistful look she said, "I thought so."

It was obvious that God had gone before me and taken care of me by having me fast, but I wonder if He had also gone before this nurse in order to touch her heart. After all—He *is* an amazing God!

Let's Pray:

Dear Lord, thank you for loving me and walking with me every day and every step of the way. Thank you also for "going before" me and protecting me—even when I am not aware of it. Teach me how to listen and obey your voice—even when I don't understand. Guide me in what to say, what to pray, where to go, and when to fast. Help me rest in your love and care for me. In Jesus' Name...Amen!

Reflections:

_____

_____

_____

_____

_____

_____

_____

_____

_____

The Music of Love

A couple of years into our marriage my husband Joe began working as a corrections officer at the county jail. Since he worked the night shift, my neighbors were often my security and companionship. That is why I had made it a point to pray for "my neighbors to be" whenever I heard of an upcoming vacancy in our apartment complex. We had been surrounded with pleasant, fun-loving, and relatively quiet folks—until *they* moved in!

The first clue that something was amiss was the strong odor of marijuana in my babies' room. I covered the outlets with duct tape hoping that it would eliminate the problem. But the putrid, sweet smell, though lessened, continued to permeate the atmosphere, plaguing our infant and toddler with scratchy throats and sinus problems.

Then—the traffic began. The steady stream of people parading in and out all hours of the day and night, often accompanied by loud music and slamming doors, annoyed me. But the crème de le crème was when the new occupants began to host Wiccan coven meetings.

One night, as I was watching TV with my little ones, a dark presence seemed to permeate our apartment. My two-year-old methodically rose to his feet, raised his hands, and began walking around the room calling on the name of Jesus. That did it! I knew that I had to take action—and quickly! I asked the Lord to show me what was going on. And When God told me that it was a spirit of witchcraft, I pretty much freaked out.

Now, you have to realize, although I had been a Christian since childhood, I was a brand new babe when it came to understanding spiritual warfare. I had recently read Frank Peretti's bestseller, *This Present Darkness*, which had given me some insight on my past experiences and fear issues, but I wasn't prepared for this! With my adrenaline pumping full speed ahead, I was definitely operating in the fight or flight syndrome. So being the brave soul that I was at age 25, I chose the latter and flew the coop with my little chickadees in tow.

After spending the night at a relative's house, I realized the next morning that I had to go home and *face the music*. Thankfully, the circumstances of the previous night didn't seem so ominous in the light of day. However, I still didn't have a clue as to what I should do. Since I didn't think I had enough evidence to call the police about the apparent drug use, and practicing witchcraft wasn't illegal, I decided to take my grievances to the authority I knew the best—God.

When the kids and I arrived back at the apartment, I

went in my room and called the meeting to order. It went something like this: "God, haven't I always prayed for my neighbors-to-be? Don't get me wrong. So far you have done a great job." (Unfortunately, that was my attempt at practicing thankfulness.) I then continued to reverently explain how for some reason things didn't *quite* work out this time. Of course, I was hinting that there was a mistake, and I really didn't think it was on *my* end.

Since I had absolutely no understanding of *being real* with God back in those days, I choose my words carefully as I continued to explain my uncomfortable circumstances (as if He didn't know) and culminated my rhetoric with "What are *they* doing here?" The reply I received was quick and to the point, *"I put them there, and you are not doing what I have called you to do!"*

"What? ME?! DOING WHAT?!" My mind couldn't even compute. Could it be that God deliberately placed drug dealers and witches in the apartment directly below me? It just didn't make sense! Why would He put them there, and what was *I* supposed to do about it?

As I stood there completely bewildered, God immediately impressed upon my heart that I was to go and talk to my neighbors about the spirit of witchcraft that had been revealed to me the night before. Terror gripped me as visions of murder (mine) and a subsequent funeral (mine also) ran through my head. I kissed my babies goodbye (thinking it might be for the last time) as I tucked them in for their naps. Then I opened the door where my husband lay sleeping so he could hear them if they awoke. After that, I dedicated my life to the cause of Christ and stepped out onto the porch. I was being a bit overly dramatic, I know, but you have to understand—I really thought I was going to die!

I reluctantly sauntered down the stairs completely terrified of what was about to transpire. As I lightly knocked on my neighbor's door, I inwardly was hoping that no one was home. However, anticipation of their absence quickly vanished when a tall, slender, young man in his early twenties answered the door. He was clean-cut with short dark hair, and introduced himself as John. He was soon accompanied by his roommate Jimmy. Jimmy was also slender, but he was younger and had light-brown shoulder-length hair.

After introducing myself, to my own disbelief, I blurted out, "Who did you have over last night?" Both John and Jimmy looked at each other quizzically. "Then once more I found myself speaking with a boldness I knew was not of me: "God told me that there was a spirit of witchcraft here."

It was then that John replied, "Uhh—well, that is because we were having our coven meeting here." Before I could even assimilate the new data, I spoke out in intrepidness. "Don't you know that witchcraft is of Satan?" John stepped back while simultaneously shaking his head in disagreement. He then began to explain that although he used to be into black magic, he was now into white magic, concluding that instead of worshipping

Satan, he now worshipped the sun god "Rah" and there was nothing evil in that. Again, I found myself countering, "If what you are doing is not evil then how come my Jesus told me about the spirit of witchcraft here?" Neither John nor Jimmy responded.

My fear being gone, I informed John and Jimmy, or maybe a better expression would be *warned* them, that I had to cover the outlets in my babies' room because of the marijuana smoke, and further advised them that they might reconsider their actions since they lived beneath a corrections officer. After exchanging worried glances, they agreed, apologized, and then politely closed the door. I returned to my apartment, not only very much alive, but also totally amazed at the courage God had given a chicken-hearted woman like me.

Not only was I encouraged by the personal victory I had won, but I was also relieved that I had completed my *little assignment,* and I breathed a sigh of relief as I went in to check on my sleeping babies. It was a wonderful feeling to know that my part was over—or so I thought. However, I was soon to discover that God had other plans, and my role in those plans had just begun.

The Lord has a way of burdening our hearts for the lost, and mine became deeply burdened. Many a night I was jolted out of a sound sleep by those guys downstairs. Sometimes it was because of the ruckus going on, which was definitely motivation to pray. But more often, it was because I was being called to intercede. Lying on my living room floor, I would fervently pray for them individually as God would lay their struggles on my heart.

As I uttered up prayers for John and Jimmy's salvation, their protection, their freedom, their deliverance, and their futures, the Lord opened up my heart to their hurts and disappointments, and I began to really care about them. It was during one of these nights of intercession that God showed me something He wanted me to do. The agony of the request cut me to the core.

Over the next few weeks, I tried to convince myself I had misheard. But no matter how much I tried to block them out, the words continued to work their way to the forefront of my thoughts, until they had crept their way into my heart. Once there, they continued to stir until there was no longer any doubt. The only question was when?

I stood alone on my balcony in the stillness of the night, rehearsing the events of the past few weeks. It had seemed like everything had been going so well. Not only had I had many opportunities to talk to John and Jimmy while playing outside with the kids in the evenings, but I was encouraged about some of our conversations, at least until that morning.

The previous afternoon my husband had had "the boys," as I affectionately called them, arrested for growing pot in their yard, and in the morning, we had discovered that our car tires had been slashed. My hopes in believing that maybe there was a purpose in "the boys" living below us had been dashed. I had started doubting everything! Feeling anger surging, I had decided to go for a walk to cool off and clear my head. My heart had been aching as I thought about how quickly my friends had become my foes.

I had been convinced that certainly after all that had transpired, God would have released me from what He had laid on my heart to do weeks before. However, as I briskly walked around the complex, no release had been given, and once again the Holy Spirit had begun to speak to my heart, *"You have been asking me what it means to love people and to see them through My eyes."* Then I had heard it again, *"Give Jimmy your guitar."*

My guitar—my most prized possession, and the only thing I owned of monetary value. My guitar—my beautiful twelve string with the slender neck that I could actually wrap my hand around! My guitar—my treasured gift from God! I had rejoiced when I had finally received it after almost a decade of waiting. It had already become my faithful companion, although I was still just beginning to learn how to play it— and now I was supposed to give it away—not even to a friend—but to my enemy!

Since afternoon, I had been waiting for the right time, and now, standing on the balcony I knew that time had arrived. I can't even remember all of the emotions that were going through my mind as I stood outside that night cradling my guitar in my arms. I think I was secretly hoping like Abraham with Isaac, that it was some kind of test, and at the last minute God would place a ram in the thicket to release me.

I could feel the music from the downstairs apartment vibrating under my feet as I leaned over the balcony to observe the surroundings. There were about five young men hanging out in the yard below. I silently prayed, "Lord, if everyone goes inside but Jimmy then I *know* this is you." Within minutes, the yard cleared, except for Jimmy. He was standing against the fence. Reluctantly, I leaned over the railing and said, "Jimmy, I have a gift for you." Then feeling as though I was losing my very best friend, I firmly grasped the neck of my guitar and lowered it over the balcony. Jimmy looked up in total amazement, held up his hands, and took hold of the curved body. His eyes then began to water. Having obvious difficulty in expressing himself, he managed to slowly mouth the words, "For—for me? No one has ever given me anything before."

I explained that the guitar was a gift from Jesus. I told him that I had been led to give it to him because Jesus wanted him to know that He loved him, and that He had a plan for his life. After Jimmy expressed his thanks, I turned around and went inside. However, to my amazement, I was not grieving. Just moments before, I thought that this night would end in sorrow, but as I walked back into the apartment, waves of joy began to flood over me—more joy than I had ever experienced in my lifetime! I had been blessed to be able to experience a glimpse of the Lord's love for another, and music poured into my soul—sweet music—beautiful music—the *music of love*!

I can't tell you what happened after that because John and Jimmy were evicted for some other offenses. But some time later, while I was praying, I saw a vision of a young man with light-brown shoulder-length hair. He was on a mission field worshipping the Lord with all of his heart. In his arms he was cradling a beautiful twelve string guitar. As he sang and strummed, music was pouring out to those around him; not just an audible melody, but a supernatural symphony—sweet music—beautiful music—the *music of God's redeeming love!*

♥ *Heart Encounter* ♥

1. It's so easy to see people through our own eyes and to judge them accordingly. Although God hates sin, He loves the sinner. Romans 5:8 tells us that Christ died for us while we were yet sinners. What does this scripture mean to you?

2. I love the account in John chapter 4, when Jesus encounters the woman at the well. There have been times in my life when I have felt like that woman—confused, unworthy, and alone. Although Jesus shows her that He is aware of who she is and what she is

doing, He does not dwell on her flaws. Instead, He offers her Himself, the *living water*. Do you believe that no matter what you have done, or currently are doing, Jesus loves you and offers Himself to you?

3. That this woman had had five husbands and was currently living with a man shows that she had spent her life attempting to quench her thirst for love and acceptance. Have you ever found yourself trying to drink from relationships or things of this world in an attempt to satiate your parched soul? Explain.

4. When Jesus told her of the *living water* that would keep her from thirsting again, she could not think beyond her own understanding. She wanted comfort. It was a long way to the well and I'm sure it was wearisome to draw water day after day. So many times I find myself only looking for temporal relief when God is offering me things that are eternal. Do you ever find yourself doing the same?

5. When the Lord first led me to pray for John and Jimmy, my heart toward them began to change. Just as Jesus knew the heart of the woman at the well, He knows the hearts of others. As you and I spend time with the Lord, He will give us His heart and show us

how to pray—not just for our friends, but also for our enemies.

6. I once had a neighbor, who was having a very difficult time with a woman in our neighborhood, so I suggested that she pray for the woman and ask God what to do. The next morning she met me outside where she informed me that God told her that she was to make her enemy a cake. When I got excited about her hearing the Lord, she caught me off guard and responded, "There's no way I'm going to make that woman a cake!" Needless to say, she didn't get a victory. Can you think of a time when the Lord may have told you to do something nice for an enemy? What was the result of either your obedience or disobedience?

7. I can't say that I have always had the right heart toward my enemies, and when I have had the right heart, it's only because God has broken me. Each time He has broken me, there is usually a cost involved, even if it is just in my laying down my pride, my rights, or my own understanding. Can you relate? Explain.

Jesus sets the ultimate example for us in that He died

for us while we were still His enemies. Knowing His heart will transform our hearts and make us instruments that bless others and give us the grace to *love* our enemies and to *do good* to those who despitefully use us. As we carry His unconditional love to the world, even the most conflicting chaos can become melodious as Heaven sings the beautiful music of God's love through our lives.

Let's Pray:

Precious Lord, thank you for dying for me while I was still your enemy. I know that you love me no matter what. Lord, fill my heart with *Your* love for those around me; for my friends as well as for my enemies. Bless me to be a blessing and make me an instrument so I can play a part in your beautiful symphony. In Jesus' Name…Amen!

Reflections:

_____

_____

_____

_____

_____

_____

_____

_____

Blooming Time

The chain of events that led up to my husband getting his first full-time police officer position not only stretched me, but made me wonder if I had totally lost my mind.

After putting the kids to bed one night, the Lord directed me through each room of the house and instructed me to get rid of things. I'm not talking about a *few* items either. Apparently, we were getting ready to "clean house" on a grand scale. There was just *one* little problem—I didn't know how to tell my husband. How do you tell a man who gets angry when God's name is even mentioned that God said we are supposed to get rid of our furniture? The answer is—you don't! You let God do it instead. With that in mind, I prayed, "Lord, if this is *You*, bring Joe into agreement. Amen!"

When Joe arrived home later that night, he went from room to room loudly expressing his hatred for our furniture. I was shocked! Since we didn't have money to buy new shoes much less furnishings, it was pretty obvious that God was directing Joe without him realizing it.

Joe and I had been hoping the local sheriff's department would hire him. But the morning he went to test for the position, I felt led to have an impromptu yard sale in which I sold all of the furniture we had talked about getting rid of a few days before. Little did either of us know that we were being prepared for a quick *big move* in which we would not be able to take much with us. When Joe returned home that afternoon and saw our duplex was pretty much empty, he commented, "Well, I guess you don't think I'm going to get the job." He didn't. A few weeks later he was offered a position in another city. Our step in faith of selling just about everything ended up not only being necessary, but it also became a testimony to our family, friends, and neighbors.

A couple of years later I was ready for another move. Although the Lord's leading had been obvious during our last move, I hadn't *exactly* gone rejoicing. It was more like inwardly kicking and screaming. But after receiving too many confirmations to not bail out, I made an agreement with God (my agreement, *not His*) in which I conceded to go to *that despicable wasteland* for two years.

The two years were now up, and I was missing my family and friends. I also felt isolated since we were fifty miles from the nearest mall or craft store. The real clincher, however, was our car situation. If I wanted to use the car, I had to drive Joe to his work almost 40 minutes away and pick him up at ungodly hours. I dreaded the fact that I had to wake up our four small children at 10:00 p.m. and sometimes not be able to return them to their beds until two or three in the morning, due to late calls or unfinished departmental paperwork. With these and a few other factors involved, it seemed like moving would be the best scenario. I had *done my time* and my heart was set on going back to Texas.

In the past, *God* had initiated *me* packing. But this time, after rehearsing my agreement, *I* told *Him* that *I* wanted to move, which seemed reason enough for me to proceed. So once I received Joe's consent, I readily attacked our small storage in the carport to prepare for the influx of new boxes. In accordance with our previous moves, I began sorting, wrapping, and filling box after box, only leaving out the necessities that would allow us to function for a few weeks. Once I finished packing, I then set about telling the whole world (at least it seemed like the *whole* world) that we were going to be moving soon, because if you're going to make a first class fool out of yourself, you might as well have a fan club cheering you on!

Since our last move had been a testimony, I made sure that I let everybody, and I mean *everybody*, (friends, neighbors, relatives, store personnel—my whole church), in the area know that we were moving. After all, it was only fitting that *I*, as God's obedient servant, be solely responsible for making sure He would get all of the glory possible from this situation. But after a month passed, I started to get a *little* anxious. Not only were there no unforeseen calls for job opportunities or green lights for relocation to Texas, there were no changes at all. People were starting to question why we were still around. I began to feel like an idiot.

One Sunday at church, there was a stirring in my heart to go up front during altar time. "Is there anything that you need to lay down?" the preacher beckoned. "Come to the altar and give it to Jesus!"

As I knelt on the floor pouring out *my* plans, God spoke to my heart: *"Can I use you where you are living a little while longer?"*

I was startled. "WHAT?!"

Then I heard again: *"Can I use you where you are living a little while longer?"*

Once again, I found myself telling God, "No!" I then proceeded to explain how staying would not only ruin my reputation, but it wouldn't make Him look too great either. For some reason, God didn't buy my justification nor did He seem concerned about *His* or *my* reputation. He just gently posed the question to me again: *"Can I use you where you are living a little while longer?"* He then added, *"I need you there."*

Wow! God needed me? What a concept!

Being enlightened that there was a purpose for me living at my current residence was comforting, but I still went home reluctant. I dreaded facing the reactions as I ate humble pie—and I had a lot of it to eat. I ate slices as

I unpacked the shed, platefuls as I visited with neighbors, and whole pans of the stuff at church and while running errands around town. I thought I would never quit hearing the unwelcome words, "You're still here? I thought you were moving!"

Although, at first, they were bitter, my daily doses of humility began to take on a sweetness of their own. During the following year, I grew in my faith, was blessed with new friends, and witnessed the Lord move powerfully in my life, as well, as in the lives of some of our neighbors. Even though the lesson was difficult, I can honestly say that I am so very thankful God chose to use me there *a little while longer.*

Perhaps you have seen the famous photograph depicting a small flower growing out of a crack in cement. God is so amazing that even when everything around you seems like a never-ending field of concrete, He can still make a way for you to flourish. Whether you are living in a difficult neighborhood, working a job that frustrates you, or going through a season that seems unbearable, *REJOICE*, for God surely has a purpose. As you submit your situation to Him, *He* will open the right doors at the right time. But in the meantime, continue to put down your roots, reach out, and *bloom* where you are planted.

♥ *Heart Encounter* ♥

1. Read Esther 4:14. What wisdom does Mordecai give Esther?

2. Esther was in an extremely difficult situation. What are some difficulties facing you right now?

3. Did you think it was by accident that Esther was in the king's palace, or do you believe as Mordecai believed that she was put there for a purpose?

4. Do you think where you are placed is by accident, or like Esther, has God put you there with a specific purpose in mind? Explain.

5. Matthew 5:16 tells us, " Let your light so shine before men, that they may see your good works and glorify your Father in heaven." Ecclesiastes 9:10 also encourages, "Whatever your hand finds to do, do *it* with (ALL) your might..." How can these two scriptures apply to your current circumstances?

We are the Lord's hands, His feet, and His mouthpieces. Who knows? You may, like Esther, be positioned *for such a time as this*, for the *saving of many lives.* As you continue to be faithful and trust God in your present circumstances, He will grow you, keep you, and give you opportunities—until *He* releases you into a new season.

Let's Pray:

Lord, I put my trust in you. If it is your will to keep me where I am, give me grace, strengthen me, and anoint me to do all that you have planned for me in this place, during this time. If it is your will to move me, then move heaven and earth on my behalf and bring me to the place that is *your best* for me. I want to live where you want me to live, work where you want me to work, and worship where you want me to worship. I want to live my life for you and shine for you. I want to be a blessing to others. Let me be your hands, your feet, and your mouthpiece to those around me. Yes, Sweet Jesus, help me to bloom! In Jesus' Name…Amen!

Reflections:

_____
_____
_____
_____
_____
_____
_____
_____
_____

Graven Images

*W*hen a friend mentioned he had attended a study about *Praying with an Idol in Your Heart*, conviction hit me like a ton of bricks. In the courtroom of my soul, the gavel had fallen and I was pronounced "Guilty!" I cringed as I thought about all of the times I have come before the Lord with an invisible sticky note listing my unmet desires pasted on my forehead. Many of those times, I cried out to God thinking I was in *faith*. In reality, I was driven out of *fear* because I couldn't bear to think of living without the thing or outcome that I was desiring come to pass. Consequently, through the years, and some *not so fun* experiences, I have learned there is a huge difference between being broken (being led by the Lord) and being driven (a fleshly attempt to lead the Lord). True brokenness reveals our hearts and releases us to trust the heart of God, thus birthing life. Being driven causes us to take control and hold on tightly because we can't bear to suffer loss or let go of a longing—thus, breeding death.

When the image you and I are lifting up in our hearts is greater than our image of God, we are praying with an idol in our heart. Idols can take on many forms. They can be physical graven images, false deities, or even people. They can be obvious outwardly destructive vices like drugs, sex, and alcohol, or they can manifest inwardly, such as the love of money, appearance, position, or power. The list can go on and on. Virtually anything or anyone you and I place in a high position in our lives has the potential of becoming an idol. However, I have discovered the most difficult idols to recognize are the ones that are *hidden* in our hearts.

Hidden idols often develop from good intentions. Praying for our lost loved ones to come to Christ, petitioning for the safety of our children, standing in faith for healing, trusting for damaged relationships to be repaired, or believing for our failing marriage to be restored, are all good things in and of themselves. But even the *good things* can lead us into idolatry when you and I cross the line from intercession to obsession.

Although it is right to believe the Lord for miracles in our lives and in the lives of our loved ones, you and I need to be careful that we are not consumed by our desires. Being consumed by our desires keeps us from trusting God. While it is important and even scriptural to fervently pray for needs and desires for ourselves and for others, it is also equally important to lay everything and everyone on the altar and trust God with the outcome. Powerful prayer is marked by position, passion, and purpose—not possession.

Trust takes the outcome out of our hands and places it in the Lord's hands. Instead of trusting the Lord through prayer, idolatry causes us to use prayer as a means to get to a specific end. Can you and I come before the Lord alone without continuously bringing these people, wants, and desires with us? If not, that may be a good indication that we are not praying with pure motives or heart. Our motivation for prayer becomes perverse when our desires become the continual focus of our lives.

I remember when I continued to believe and pray for my broken marriage to be restored. I loved my husband, and I couldn't bear the thought of going through a divorce. I was also bound by a lie of the enemy telling me that God would disqualify me from serving Him if my marriage didn't succeed. I was convinced that if I continued to pray, fast, declare, and believe, my husband would surrender his life to Christ and our marriage would be saved. I even went as far as setting up a little Jericho made from blocks in my living room and declaring that the walls would come down.

Now, nothing is wrong with such prophetic acts if they are led by the Lord. You and I are supposed to take authority in situations, but I had crossed the line from intercession into obsession. During every waking hour and even throughout the night I was so consumed with the deterioration of my children's and my futures, that I couldn't bring myself to comprehend an alternate outcome.

There was a season when I had prayed for my husband out of brokenness. I felt his pain and my heart desired for him to know Christ and be free. But what I was experiencing at this time was different. Instead of brokenness, which would have brought me to a place of surrender, I was becoming obsessed, which brought me to a place of selfishness. I wanted what I wanted, and I could not comprehend otherwise. I was convinced that neither my children nor I would be "okay" if things didn't turn out as planned, and I was determined to see those plans come to pass.

One Sunday when I was praying at the altar I saw a vision. I was running across a football field clutching a football. As I looked down, I saw my husband superimposed on the ball. I was determined to carry him across the goal line. As I continued to *go for a touchdown* Jesus stood in front of me holding out his hands and very gently said, *"Give me the ball."* I stopped dead in my tracks and began to argue with Him, "Lord, I can't. I've carried him for sixteen years. I've prayed. I believed. I have *got* to take him over the line." Notice all of the **I's**. There is a reason it is called **"I"** dolatry. Jesus calmly shook his head and repeated, *"Give me the ball."* Reluctantly, I handed Him the ball. Then He pointed to the bleachers and instructed me to sit down and watch the game. I went home that day realizing I needed to make a conscious effort to give the ball (my husband) to the Lord. Although the final outcome of the game didn't turn out the way I had planned, it eventually turned out with more touchdowns than I had expected.

Praying with an idol in our hearts will also rob us of our peace. In being consumed by my circumstances, I lost my peace. Not only was I in constant turmoil, I had difficulty eating and sleeping. When my 5'8" frame got down to 98 pounds I called a friend for help. I asked her to pray against the nausea so I would have an appetite. But instead, she prayed that I would have peace. When you and I realize that we have lost our peace, we need to stop and seek the Lord and ask Him to show us where, when, and why we lost it. It will almost always have something to do with trust. Then we might want to check our hearts for idols.

Deception is also often interlinked with idolatry. When we are in idolatry we will see what we want to see and hear what we want to hear—then act accordingly. Although, there were serious problems throughout my marriage, my idolatry caused me to be deceived. Even when others tried to set me straight I wouldn't listen, because I was convinced that the outcome would be worth it all. I see this often, especially in abusive situations.

Once when I was praying for a woman who was in a situation much worse than mine had been, the Lord gave me a vision. I saw her bowing down and laying sacrifices before her husband. Immediately, I was reminded of a video clip I had watched revealing how some tribes in Africa sacrifice chickens to the demons to try to get them to leave them alone. When a person is being abused, verbally, mentally, emotionally, or physically, he or she will often try to placate the abuser in order to bring a semblance of peace.

I used to believe that peace was the absence of conflict. Some conflict is good; some external peace is not. *False peace* will either cause us to live in denial or teach us to revolve our whole world around a temperamental or controlling person, which is nothing more than idolatry. Unfortunately, while it is easy to see the controlling nature of the abuser, the "abusee" rarely sees the controlling side of him/herself. Peace is characterized by a soul at rest; not a situation that is momentarily quiet. Unknowingly, "abusees" fear man more than they trust God.

Warped definitions of love can also lead us into idolatry. When we define love as constant worrying or not being able to live without another person, or if our definition of love strips us of our value, we should check our hearts for idols. My definition of love was birthed out of a martyr mentality. I would lay down all I was for the sake of another human being. The truth is that I saw no value in myself, and had no clue as to *who* I was in Christ. I carried this mentality for years. One morning, the Lord woke me up and said, *"Allowing your husband to be a tyrant is **not** loving him. True love is when two people help each other become the best they can be."* Then He told me that it was time to practice *tough love*. I had no clue what *tough love* was, but by God's grace, a neighbor being led of the Lord stopped by that afternoon and gave me some tapes. They were the *Love Must Be Tough* series by Dr. James Dobson. By the end of the day I was starting to *get a clue.*

Idolatry steals our joy. Nehemiah reminds the people that "the joy of the Lord is our strength" (Nehemiah 8:10). Since joy can't be determined by a reliance on things, the actions of others, or the outcome of situations, you and I need to honestly ask ourselves if we can be content in Christ regardless of our circumstances. Anything or anyone can be taken from our lives at anytime. Jesus is our only constant. Being content does not mean being void of emotion or desires. Contentment is the assurance that no matter what happens, we can trust God to provide for us, be with us, and see us through.

It is difficult to understand a loving relationship with God when we are praying with an idol in our heart. Either we will view God as an ogre who is withholding from us, or we will view Him as a *Sugar Daddy* who will give us everything we want if we beg Him enough. The reality is God is a *loving Father* who desires for us to know Him intimately. He desires to bless us more than we can ever think or imagine. However, sometimes those blessings will come in strangely wrapped packages.

The enemy comes to kill, steal, and destroy, but God comes to bring abundant life. Whether our idols take on the form of noticeable destructive vices, such as drugs or alcohol, or less noticeable forms, such as greed, power, unhealthy relationships, or unmet desires, you and I are being stolen from. Idolatry brings turmoil, but surrender and trust bring peace and joy in abundance.

I am so very thankful that the Lord is our portion. He is our strength and our strong tower. He is truly all you and I need. As we come before Him and seek His kingdom everything else will fall into place. The more I grow, the more the idols in my life are exposed. As I go before the altar sometimes clenching my idols tightly in my fists, I have to choose to lay them down. It is then I hear the sweet voice of the Spirit whisper in my ear, *"Do you really trust me?"* Often, in that place, the only prayer I can offer is the one the man with the epileptic son spoke over two thousand years ago, "Lord, I believe; help my unbelief!" (Mark 9:24). But it's enough to unclench my fingers and release me toward abundance.

♥ *Heart Encounter* ♥

1. In Judges 6:25 Gideon is instructed by an angel of the Lord to tear down his father's idols. The Word tells us that although he did as he was told, he did it at night because he was afraid. Fear will keep us in idolatry; whether it is the fear of someone, fear of consequences, or the fear of loss. Can you think of a time when fear kept you in idolatry?

2. Notice that although Gideon was afraid, he was still obedient. I used to be paralyzed by fear, so much so that there was a season I was terrified to be alone in my house. Through a process of learning truth, receiving good teaching, and a whole lot of prayer, I had to learn to walk toward what I feared instead of running away from it. Can you think of a time when you received victory by facing your fears, even if it was under the cloak of night?

3. God is faithful and merciful. When He gives you and me revelation and instructs us to tear down our idols, He often bring others to help us. Read Judges 6:27. Did Gideon tear down the altar of Baal and the Asherah alone? Who went with him?

4. Before Gideon was instructed to tear down the idols, he had already spent a little bit of time with the angel of the Lord. The angel had informed him that he (Gideon) was the one God was going to use to save Midian. Before this daytime meeting with the angel ended, Judges 6:23 tells us that the angel said to him, "Peace be to you, do not fear; you shall not die" (AMP). Later that night Gideon was instructed to tear down the idols. In the process of tearing down the idols in our lives you and I sometimes will feel as though we are going to die. How can the words

spoken by the angel to Gideon long ago comfort and encourage us as we face our own idolatry?

The enemy comes to kill, steal, and destroy, but God comes to bring life and that in abundance. There were consequences when Gideon destroyed the idols—even his life was threatened. But God kept him according to the promise given him. "But the Spirit of the Lord clothed Gideon with Himself *and* took possession of him" Judges 6:34 (AMP).Wow! That sounds like abundance to me! Like Gideon blowing the trumpet, it makes me want to shout, "Tear down my idols, Lord, and fill me with more of you!"

Let's Pray:

Precious Lord, I thank you that you always know what is best for me. Forgive me for making other things, people, and desires more important than you. I want freedom! I'm tired of the enemy robbing from my life. I choose to have no other gods besides you. Shine the searchlight of your Holy Spirit into my heart and reveal any idols that are residing there. Give me wisdom and courage to tear down the graven images that have stolen from me, and pour out your abundance into my life. I thank you for the freedom you have promised me, and I take hold of it by faith knowing that you will bring it to pass! In Jesus' Name…Amen!

Reflections:

_____

_____

_____

_____

_____

_____

_____

_____

_____

A Froggy Tale

 M any of you have heard the saying, "The spirit is willing, but the flesh is weak." However, I think there are times when, although our flesh is weak, we convince ourselves that we have willing spirits—even when we don't. One such time for me was when I was led to visit the home of some people who were going through tremendous trials.

As soon as I arrived, I set to work cleaning—both physically and spiritually. As I praised, prayed, and scrubbed, all was going well until I pulled back the shower curtain in the master bath to expose a large, dead frog lying in the middle of the tub. I shrieked and jumped back. When I cautiously approached the tub again—just to sneak a peek—I realized upon closer examination (but not too close) that this creature with its shriveled body and bulging eyes was not a newcomer to its porcelain sepulcher. Being both curious and disgusted, I approached the lady of the house and asked her about the circumstances surrounding the frog's demise. To say the least, I was a bit surprised when she explained that the frog had already been in the tub when they moved into the house several months before. "We don't use that bath tub," she said, "because no one wants to remove the disgusting thing."

Although her explanation was a little bizarre, it satisfied my curiosity so I retreated back to the bathroom with the intention of cleaning everything, except the tub. But, as I resumed my work, I heard the Holy Spirit speak to my heart: *"Take the frog out of the bathtub."*

Now, you probably realize from previous stories I wasn't going to touch that thing without a little discussion. So I pulled out my Genesis 22 bargaining chip. Since I was aware that sometimes, like in the account of Abraham's sacrifice of Isaac, God just wants to test our willingness and then releases the burden and makes another way, I figured I'd give it a try. I'm not sure what that way would have been since there is no such thing as a Dead Amphibian Waste Removal Company, but wisdom is rarely at play when we're in the midst of a battle. And since I just knew I would retch if I had to scrape the putrid remains from the tub, declaring my willingness seemed to be my only option. So I set about making myself willing.

"Okay, Lord, I'm willing."

The words sounded good and full of surrender. I not so patiently waited for affirmation that my "willingness" was all that was required; thus, signifying my release.

But in my heart I heard: *"Good, now remove the frog."*

"No! No! You don't understand, Lord. I *said* I was willing!"

"I'm glad you are willing," He responded. *"Now, remove the frog."*

Not only was the scenario not playing out the way I had planned, it had now become very obvious that neither my spirit nor my flesh were willing participants. Since saying the words did not signify my willingness on either part, there was nothing left to do but to bring both under submission and remove the frog.

Just so you know, the frog didn't come up easily, and, yes, it was disgusting. I had to pry and scrape and then clean up the cemented skin residue. But our flesh doesn't always die easily either. However, despite my weaknesses, God gave me the grace to complete the task with the contents of my stomach intact, and I was once again reminded that, "I can do all things through Christ who strengthens me!"

How many times, like in my situation with the frog, do you and I convince ourselves that saying the right words indicate a willing spirit? Sometimes, in order to overcome a battle with our flesh, we might have to do some soul searching. Just as I had to remove that dead frog from the bathtub, there might be some things "of death" in our lives that we need to remove as well. In Psalm 139:23 David says, "Search me [thoroughly], O God, and know my heart! Try me and know my thoughts!"(AMP). Maybe there are some areas in your life in which you are struggling. If so, I would encourage you to be honest with yourself and with God and ask if your spirit is "really willing." However, be prepared to take action if you don't get the reply you were hoping for.

♥ Heart Encounter ♥

1. Is there something of death in your life that needs to be cleaned up? If so, name it.

2. Our spirits must be willing in order to bring our flesh under submission. Have you told yourself your spirit is willing, but your flesh is weak concerning an area of temptation? Is your spirit *really* willing?

3. When I was being convicted to clean up the frog, I thought that just saying the words would signify willingness. Do you believe that words are enough to overcome or do they also have to be backed up with actions?

4. In Romans 7:13-25 Paul shares his struggle with his sin nature. Over and over again he expresses how he

does the very things he does not want to do. I have heard some people use this as an excuse to continue in deliberate sin by declaring, "Oh, I just can't help it!" Do you think that Paul is justifying his sin by acknowledging his weak flesh?

5. While it is true that you and I have weak areas and there are some battles that will not be won easily; surrendering to the Lord brings us victory. What does surrender mean to you? Do you think that surrender is active or passive? Does surrender mean to just roll over and give in? Write your definition of surrender.

6. There is a world of difference between giving up (admitting we are weak and giving the battle to the Lord) and giving in. Giving up places us under God's authority; while giving in opens us up to the enemy. God's grace comes in abundance when we surrender before Him. But self-pity, condemnation, and hopelessness come in and torment us when we roll over and refuse to deal with our wrong choices and harmful patterns. Can you think of a time when you gave up and surrendered the battle you were facing to God? What was the result? Can you think of a time when you just gave in because it was just "too hard?" What was the result of that decision?

Removing the frog from a bathtub might have been a simple, trivial thing, but it opened my understanding to other areas in my life where I needed to submit. Once I realized there were battles I was ignoring, I had to choose to face them, examine my heart for willingness, and then surrender and obey. When you and I surrender, God picks us up, clothes us with heavenly armor, and prepares us for battle. But when we give into our flesh, we are left lying on the ground naked and vulnerable to the enemy's attacks. The victory is definitely in surrender.

Let's Pray:

Dear Lord, thank you for paying for all my sins through the precious blood of Jesus. I give up and surrender all that I have and all that I am to you. Reveal areas of my life where my spirit has not been willing, and give me the grace to take action and deal with my unhealthy mindsets and patterns. Clothe me with your armor and equip me for the battle at hand; for in my weakness you are surely strong. Although I know in and of myself that I can do nothing, Philippians 4:13 tells me that "I can do all things through Christ Jesus who strengthens me." I love you Lord! You are my strength, my hope, and my life! In Jesus' Name…Amen!

Reflections:

_____

_____

_____

_____

_____

_____

_____

_____

_____

Grounded

*I*n his mid-teens one of my sons decided to make life difficult for me so I would release him to go and live elsewhere. His plan worked! Actually it worked so well that almost a year later when he asked to come back home I was apprehensive.

A couple of nights after my son's request to return I had a dream. In my dream I had just returned home after being separated from my baby boy for nine months. He was now over a year old. Although I immediately stepped back into the role of his mother, I felt no connection to my baby. However, as I methodically changed my baby and took care of his needs, my heart softened. My feelings of alienation changed to adoration. By the end of my dream I longed to "make up" for all of the time I had lost with my precious baby son during my absence.

When I awoke, I kept hearing in my spirit, *"Delight in your son! Delight in your son! Delight in your son!"*

Since delight wasn't even close to the emotions I was feeling for my son at that time, I asked the Lord to help me see my son through His eyes. He did! Within days, aggravation and apprehension turned to adoration. By the time my son moved back home, I truly delighted in him, though, at times, I still wanted to string "my precious man-child" up by his toes.

Within weeks of his return home, I discovered that my son had made a less than wise decision (to put it lightly). I retreated to my room for counsel. As I poured out my disappointment and anger to God about the current situation and sought wisdom as to how to handle it, God gently spoke to my heart: *"The baby has a dirty diaper. Change the diaper."* I remembered how my toddlers had often objected to diaper changes because they didn't want their play time interrupted, and I started to laugh. Then I asked the Lord to show me what sort of uncomfortable "diaper change" my son needed. Armed with new insight and attitude I went to my son and told him how much he meant to me. Then I grounded him.

Over the course of the next couple of years my "precious boy" was grounded often. I think there were times he saw the four walls of his room more than his classroom. But since God had taught me how to "delight in my son" I no longer took his behavior personally. I could separate who he was (love the sinner) from what he did (hate the sin).

Whenever I caught him making wrong choices I would smile and say, "You are so adorable—and you are *so* grounded!" He heard the line so often, he started finishing my sentence.

As I learned to separate my son's behavior from his being I learned something new about the heart of Father God. I learned that when we mess up and make less than wise decisions, God doesn't stand over us raging like a bull with smoke coming out of His nostrils, pronouncing how terrible we are. Instead He looks at us with love in His eyes and says, *"Baby, you are so adorable—and you are so grounded."*

♥ *Heart Encounter* ♥

1. Why do you think God disciplines us?

2. In Hebrews 12:6, we are told that God disciplines those He loves. Healthy discipline is not so much punishment as it is redirection. I disciplined my son because I loved him and knew that he needed to change his behavior because it was detrimental to him. Can you give an example from your life where you have seen God do the same? What were the results of God's loving discipline?

3. Although discipline never *feels* good, it *is* good. What would happen if you and I let our toddlers run out into traffic? Although a toddler might not understand the danger of moving vehicles, the parent does. Do you trust that God (your parent) understands what is best—even when you don't agree?

4. God's goal in disciplining you and me is to separate us from sinful behaviors, not to separate us from Him. Sometimes when I had to take a "tough love" stance with my children they would view me as the enemy and pull away. Although I might have been tempted to change my mind so they would like me, I knew I had to stand strong. Giving in would not have been what was best for *them*. Have you ever thought of God as being your enemy? How do you view Him now?

5. We can learn a lot about God from His relationship with Israel. God longed to restore His relationship with the Israelites. But in order for Him to bring them back to Him, He had to deal with their sin. Luke 13:34 tells us God's heart in the matter. How does this passage speak to you about God's desire for relationship with you?

Since God loves us and desires relationship with us, He knows we need to grow. One afternoon, when I was addressing some of my son's concerning behaviors, I glanced at a small plant on the edge of the counter. I held up the plant and said, "Son, you are like this plant. As your mother, it is my responsibility to set boundaries (your container), water you with truth (the Word of God), surround you with dirt (love), and even put a little fertilizer (discipline) on you from time to time. But that is where my responsibility ends. You are the one who has to decide to grow." Doesn't God do the same? Are you choosing to grow?

Let's Pray:

Dear Lord, thank you for giving me boundaries through your Word. Thank you also for being a loving daddy who disciplines me (redirects me through circumstances and consequences) in order to guide me and grow me. I know that you know what is best for me, even when I don't like it. Draw me closer to your heart, and help me to trust your loving discipline. In Jesus' Name…Amen!

Reflections:

_____

_____

_____

_____

_____

_____

_____

_____

Pull the Tooth

When I think of teeth, I think of pain. When I think of dentists—well, let's not even go there! In my early twenties I suffered from severe immune system reactions that often mimicked the symptoms of multiple sclerosis. My doctor informed me that there were some case studies linking multiple sclerosis symptoms to mercury fillings and advised me to have my fillings replaced. So in one sitting, with very little anesthetic because I was so allergic, I went through a grueling afternoon in which seventeen mercury (amalgam) fillings were drilled out and replaced with temporary clove-based fillings.

At the time of the procedure, my dentist informed me that although clove-based fillings had been created for temporary use, there have been cases of them being effective for long periods of time. "I know of some Vietnam veterans who have had clove fillings for over twenty years," he remarked. "But," he cautioned, "eventually, you will need to replace them—probably with gold." Since I wasn't into having a million dollar mouth, I left his office that day mumbling through what felt like pillow-sized lips, "Yeah right. I *might* see you in twenty years!"

By that evening, I was so miserable I wasn't sure if I could wait 20 hours much less 20 years before my next dental visit. Not only did it feel as though I had peppermint candy chips permanently lodged in my teeth, the clove based fillings were so hypersensitive to hot and cold I wasn't sure which would be more torturous— eating a large bowl of ice cream or having bamboo splinters driven under my fingernails. Thankfully, the sensitivity lessoned during the following months, and I was blessed with a few years of respite—until one night when I woke up with a knife-searing pain.

Since we had moved out of state by then, I opened the phonebook and selected a new dentist. After being medicated and treated for an abscessed tooth the following day, the dentist assured me that there were no other problems. So when the relief I was anticipating continued to evade me, I resigned myself to the fact that teeth and pain were synonymous. I continued to ignore any warning signs until a year later when the entire left side of my face began to swell, giving me the resemblance of a lopsided chipmunk. I was then given full mouth X-rays that irrefutably showed that my temporary fillings had been deteriorating underneath, causing some more of my teeth to become infected. To remedy this, my clove fillings were drilled out and replaced with porcelain fillings.

Since my teeth had now been drilled three times, they were very sensitive because many of my new fillings were so deep they were connecting with nerves. In order to bring some relief, I switched to sensitive toothpaste. I also began a nightly ritual of swishing with hydrogen peroxide in order to prevent infections. But the pain continued.

A few years later, when the pain again became unbearable, I called a local dentist who prescribed antibiotics, and scheduled me with an appointment the following morning. Once again, I was given a bad report. Apparently, the porcelain fillings were so deep, they were cracking. Not only would my fillings need to be drilled out again and replaced, some of them were too far gone to save the teeth without getting root canals. Since I had limited finances I agreed to have some of the porcelain-filled teeth replaced with mercury, and some of my back teeth removed.

The first tooth came out with little effort since the roots had been dead for so long they had deteriorated. Upon extraction, the dentist held up what looked like a miniature ice cream cone, as he exclaimed, "I've never seen anything like this before!"

The next tooth—well let's just say it didn't go quite as smoothly. It felt more like my dentist was using a crowbar and a wrecking ball rather than pliers and sharp instruments to dislodge it. However, the intense pressure being exerted against my gums during the extraction was nothing compared to the pressure that was being exerted against my heart.

I had gone in that morning expecting to have my tooth pulled based on my last experience: the dentist gives you a shot, yanks a few times and *voila!* It's done! Well, I guess tooth extractions are kind of like childbirth experiences—no two come out the same way. With each failed attempt, the dentist applied more force. The more force he applied, the more uncomfortable I became. When I couldn't stand it any longer, I silently cried out. "Lord, help me! Why won't this tooth come out?" That is when the inward pressure began.

Immediately, I saw the face of someone who had hurt me during my childhood; someone who I had deliberately chosen to hate, and I heard in my spirit, *"Forgive _____."*

"I can't do that, Lord! I just can't!" I responded. As I heard the most recent dental tool scrape against my tooth, the tool of conviction scraped against my heart, and the pressure against my gums continued to increase in direct correlation with the pressure inside my soul. God was going deep, and I didn't want to go there. The dentist was going for the infected root of my tooth, but God was going for the infected root of my heart. My loving Father was saying, *"This has caused you pain long enough. You have tried to ignore it and medicate it so you could bear it, but I want to extract it. Forgive_____."*

At that point, the poor tired dentist paused to wipe the sweat from his brow and then set to work once again. He wriggled and pulled and pried some more until he finally stopped what he was doing and exclaimed, "I just don't understand! Why won't it come out?"

Well, I understood! But there was *no way* I was going to clue *him* in! Thankfully, I had a persevering dentist, and thankfully I have a persevering God, because *neither* one of them was going to let the matter go. As the dentist grabbed the pliers again, God grabbed my heart and they both began to apply more pressure in order to break the root.

"It has to let go," said the dentist. *"You have to let it go,"* said God.

"I can't take much more of this!" I thought to myself. I tried to think of other things, but the volume increased as I continued to hear in my spirit, "Forgive_____. Forgive_____. Forgive_____."

By this time, (I kid you not,) the scenario resembled a scene out of a Western comedy. The dentist had one foot up on the chair and he was pushing and pulling with all of his might, as God got a foothold in my heart and was pushing and pulling as well. I thought that I was going to come up out of my chair, but instead I came up out of my bondage. As soon as I said in my heart, "I forgive _____," the dentist yanked one last time, stumbled slightly backwards, and held up the bloody reward for his effort. It was done. The tooth was pulled. The root was extracted, and a victory was won, all in one single act of "letting go."

♥ *Heart Encounter* ♥

1. Just as the infections in my teeth were hidden from the naked eye, the bitter root of unforgiveness in my heart was often hidden. I had learned to medicate it, or even had tried to ignore it, but it was constantly causing me pain and hindrance. Can you relate? Has unforgiveness ever hindered you or caused you pain?

2. Unforgiveness can take a huge toll on us spiritually, emotionally, and physically. It can rob us of our joy; it can even rob us of our lives. In Psalms 139:14 we are told that we are "fearfully and wonderfully made." That includes how we think and how we process stress. Numerous studies have shown that unforgiveness produces negative chemicals that actually destroy the body. Unfortunately, I have experienced some of that destruction personally. How about you? Have you ever noticed a change in your heart rate, blood pressure, etc. when you think of people who have hurt you?

3. It's amazing how we can allow ourselves to be controlled even without being aware of it. I once heard a pastor say that refusing to forgive is like drinking poison and waiting for the person who has

hurt us to die. What do you think about this statement?

4. Ephesians 4:32 instructs us to "be kind to one another, tenderhearted, forgiving one another, even as God in Christ forgave you." Unforgiveness affects our hearts. The hidden infections in my teeth affected what I did and hardened me to endure more pain. The hidden infection of unforgiveness affected my actions and caused my heart to harden because of the pain. Do you believe that holding on to unforgiveness will harden your heart? If so, how?

5. In Colossians 3:12-14 we read "Therefore, as *the* elect of God, holy and beloved, put on tender mercies, kindness, humility, meekness, longsuffering; bearing with one another, and forgiving one another, if anyone has a complaint against another; even as Christ forgave you, so you also *must do*. But above all these things put on love, which is the bond of perfection." Do you believe that since Jesus forgave us when He died for our sins, He will give us the grace to forgive others who sin against us?

I don't believe that you and I can truly forgive all by ourselves. Opening our hearts and making the *choice* to forgive allows the Holy Spirit to come in and do the *work* of forgiveness. Our part is to trust and *let go;* His part is to transform our hearts through His perfect love.

I would like to clarify, however, that forgiveness does not always mean reconciliation. When you and I forgive, we release the debt against the person who has hurt us, recognizing that Christ has already shed His blood for their offense. Releasing the debt of the pain they have caused us frees us, but it does not always remove the consequences.

Even though we forgive and our hearts are changed toward our perpetrators, there will be times when you and I will still be led to bring them into accountability and/or pursue justice. Forgiveness frees us and causes us to trust the Lord, but it does not call for us to trust our perpetrators. If the Lord leads us to go to them, you and I need to ask for wisdom and go and do or say what we are led. But if not, we need to just continue to pray for them while standing back and trusting from a distance.

Let's Pray:

Dear Lord, thank you for loving me. You care for me too much to allow me to be destroyed by unforgiveness. Reveal to me anyone and everyone that I need to forgive. I know that you love all people; even those who have hurt me, so I am asking you to pull the bitter roots out of my soul that have hindered me and replace them with your love. Change my heart and my thoughts toward

_____....

Before continuing, I would encourage you to wait on the Lord for a few minutes and ask Him to reveal people you need to forgive. You may have quite a few faces and names come to mind so I have added a section on the following page to write down names.

When you are done writing, read through the rest of the prayer (Repeat the prayer for each person who came to mind.)

Sweet Jesus, I am not capable of loving _____ in my own strength so I am asking you to love him/her through me. Let me see _____through your eyes. I choose to forgive _____ for all of his/her hurtful words and behaviors. Because of your great love, I choose to bless _____.
Precious Lord, I trust *You* to heal my hurts. Forgive me for any judgments I have made. Sever any soul ties

(unhealthy connections to my mind, my will, and my emotions) that I have with _____. In Jesus' name, I take back anything that was taken from me, and give back anything that was attached to me that was not of you. I renounce the lies I believed about You (God), myself, and others because of this relationship and/or choices. Sweet Lord, fill any empty places in my heart and mind with your perfect love and truth and with the *fruits of the Spirit.* I love you, Lord! In Jesus' Name…Amen!

Lord Help Me Forgive…

_____
_____
_____
_____
_____
_____
_____

Reflections:

_____
_____
_____
_____

Deep Water

$\mathcal{A}$ friend once told me, "The more warnings, the worse the trial." I should have listened.

It seemed as though I had been sick forever. First I had whooping cough, then pneumonia, and now I was in the midst of yet another trial. As I lay in bed, my breathing labored, I seriously wondered if I was even going to make it through the night.

A few months previously, the Holy Spirit began leading me to scriptures, preparing me for a time of trial that was coming. At first I thought that if I just rebuked the enemy, the burden would be lifted. But on a daily basis I kept hearing the words: *Trust me. I'm going to take you through deep waters, the valley of the shadow of death, and a storm.*

Not only was I often led to certain passages to confirm what I was hearing in my spirit during my devotion times, but God also brought other people for confirmation as well. One was a missionary who was visiting our church. During prayer time, he looked me straight in the face and said, "Be strong and courageous and God will give you the land." After replying with a flippant "Okay," he took hold of my shoulders, met my eyes with his, and said, "No! You don't understand! You are going to have to be strong and courageous!" I remember leaving service that night asking myself, "What on earth is going to happen?"

I didn't realize that I was getting ready to enter into a period where I would be tested in a greater measure than I had ever been tested before. When the storm was finally over nothing in my life would be left intact; however, God knew, and I am forever grateful that He went before me and prepared the way in my heart, as well as in my circumstances.

When the first of many trials hit fast and furious, (although I was shaken and sifted), the Lord held me by His wondrous love. And through the dark days He continued to remind me of the promises I had been given.

I had collapsed the first time while on a G-force ride at an amusement park. After being assisted off of the ride, I sat with my daughter on a curb for almost an hour until I was able to see clearly and regain my balance. Less than a week later I collapsed in my living room. The second time I didn't fully recover, and I had been left in a position where I could barely function. I had tremendous pressure in my head, I couldn't read or write and, at times, I couldn't even remember my name. I was rarely awake and my breathing was loud and labored.

My neurologist was awaiting permission from my insurance company to schedule a CAT scan. In the meantime, my primary care doctor had diagnosed me as having emphysema, which probably resulted from my extensive bout with whooping cough a few years earlier.

Although I had experienced breathing problems ever since having whooping cough, wrong mindsets kept me from seeking further medical attention. Some mindsets were rooted in pride, but others were fear-based.

Because of his personal wounds and fears, my husband was often unsympathetic and antagonizing to anyone in our immediate or extended families who was injured or ill, so no matter what physical maladies I was struggling with, I was determined to quietly endure to prove to him that I wasn't a weakling. Besides, I was used to persevering through difficult circumstances. I was also afraid of reliving my college years and ending up in the hospital again. The underlying truth about all my messed up thinking was actually the fear of being abandoned, not just by my husband, but by God himself.

As long as I could continue to care for the kids and complete some household tasks, even though I often had to stop and sit down to catch my breath, I felt as if I had value. But now, with the new complications, I had to surrender my *I'm never going back to the doctor* attitude and resign to medical assistance. I also had to resign the care of my children over to others who graciously stepped in during my time of need.

My friends and relatives had placed me on numerous

national and international prayer chains, but I wasn't getting any better. During my brief waking moments, I would often see a vision of God's hand reaching out to me as I heard Him tell me that He loved me and that my worth was not in *what I could do,* but in *who I was.* But no matter how many times I heard God affirm me, I struggled to understand how I could be valuable in my current condition. I often thought I should just give up the fight and prepare to *go home* and be with the Lord.

On this particular night I did just that. Every noisy breath was taking such an effort, and I was tired—tired of being sick—tired of life being so hard—tired of everything. It was then that I quit breathing. I had grown accustomed to times when I could not breathe. If my inhaler wasn't handy I would gasp for air and pray until I got my next breath, but this night was different. Nothing seemed to work, and I had flat given up. As I lay on my bed unable to move, I felt as though I was fading away.

Surprisingly, all fear dissipated as three scenarios played in my head. In the first one, I went to Heaven and stayed with the Lord. I was free from all suffering and pain. It was wonderful! In the second scenario I went to Heaven and stood in front of Jesus. Jesus then said, *"It's not your time,"* and sent me back with an incredible testimony. And in the third scenario God gave me back my breath. I still felt as if I was suffocating, but since all three scenarios were winning situations, all fear was gone. I realized, no matter what, I would be victorious!

It was then I saw the vision of the *deep water*. I was

surrounded by an expansive body of it, but instead of drowning beneath the waves, Jesus was standing under the water with His hand outstretched upwardly. Where His backward flexed hand broke the surface of the water, I was peacefully laying across His palm. As peace enveloped me the vision vanished, and a drink of cool fresh air filled my lungs. I was amazed! One second I was struggling for air and the next I was breathing—still loudly—but breathing all the same. I was amazed at the goodness of God. I was amazed that He restored my breath. And I was amazed at the revelation I had received. "Wow! If this is the *deep water,*" I thought to myself, "this is incredible!" Then I went to sleep.

When I awoke the next morning, I felt a little bit stronger. The Holy Spirit spoke to my heart: *"Today is turn around day!"* I felt an urgency to get to church, so I called a friend who assisted me to the car and took me to church. When we arrived, we learned that a guest evangelist was visiting. After sitting slumped over through service, a couple of people helped me to the altar. The evangelist took one look at me and declared, "Today the Lord says, *'Everything turns around! The destruction against your body is no more! Every day, from now on, you will begin to get stronger!'*" He then continued to speak life over every organ and system in my body, beginning with my brain.

Feeling no different after prayer, I had assistance getting back home and slept for the rest of the afternoon. However, that evening I was led to go back to church.

When the altar call declared that God wanted to heal asthma and emphysema, once again I was helped to the front. But similar to what happened earlier in the day, I was taken home feeling the same as before I had left for church.

Later that night, I was lying on the living room floor by the front door because I didn't have the strength to make it back to my chair. My children sat surrounding me warily watching as I lay there taking shallow breaths. As I began to whisper in an attempt to encourage my children, I was unaware that my breathing was getting less labored, and my voice was getting clearer. Within minutes, I felt strength rise up in me and realized I was breathing strongly, deeply, and effortlessly. God had miraculously healed my lungs! My children and I rejoiced!

My doctor didn't know how to respond when I told her how I was healed, but she did admit that my lungs were functioning normally. And by the end of the following month the pressure in my head and my other concerning neurological and cardio symptoms had disappeared.

I came out of that trial stronger and healthier than I had been in years, realizing that Jesus is not only my healer, but that He is also the *Breath of Life*. Whether you and I realize it or not, every breath we take is a gift handed down from the *Father of Lights*. During the years following my bout with whooping cough (prior to my healing) when was I struggling so much to breathe, a dear woman of God once prayed that the Holy Spirit would give me breath when I couldn't breathe on my own. I took that prayer to heart. Even all these years later, I am fully aware that the Lord is literally the air that I breathe, and it is He Who gives me *breath* and *life*—even in the deepest waters.

♥ *Heart Encounter* ♥

1. Sometimes in the midst of trials we feel as if we are smothering. Has there been a time in your life when your trials seemed so heavy you felt like you had no breath? Explain.

2. How did God meet you in the midst of your trial?

3. Isaiah 43:2 encourages us that Jesus will be with us when we "pass through the waters." What should our heart posture be as Jesus holds us in the deep waters?

4. Psalms 46:10 says, "Be still, and know that I *am* God." What do these words mean to you?

5. The Bible tells us in 2 Corinthians 12:10 that in our weakness the Lord is strong. How have you seen this scripture played out in your life?

6. In the midst of my trial the Lord chose to give me back my breath and to ultimately heal my lungs; however, I realize that if He had chosen otherwise, I still would have come out a winner. Do you believe that knowing Jesus puts you in a winning situation; no matter what the outcome?

Maybe you haven't faced a situation where you could not *physically* breathe, but often, we are faced with trials where we feel as if we have *no breath*. There will be times in our lives when you and I will only be able to survive with the Holy Spirit being our oxygen. Whether we need *literal* breath or the *spiritual* breath of *life* breathed into our hearts and our circumstances, Jesus is there with full supply. In your darkest hour He will be faithful to stand in your place. Instead of letting you drown, He will give you life and hold you in the midst of the *deep waters*. Rejoice, my friend, for if you know Jesus, no matter what the outcome, yours is a win-win situation!

Let's Pray:

Precious Lord, you love me, you know me, and you hold me! It says in Romans 8:28, that nothing can separate me from your love, and in Psalm 139, that there is nowhere I can go to flee from your presence. You are in all and through all, and you are Lord of all. Thank you that even in the darkest hours when life doesn't make sense, you hold me up in the midst of the deep waters. I choose to be still and know that you are God, as I rest upon your mighty hand. For I know that no matter what the outcome—I am victoriously safe with you. In Jesus' Name...Amen!

Reflections:

_____
_____
_____
_____
_____
_____
_____
_____

A Table in the Midst

"You prepare a table before me in the presence of my enemies." Although I was well acquainted with this portion of scripture from Psalm 23, in 2008, it took on a new depth of meaning for me. Due to what the doctors deemed a misfiring in my brain, I was stuck in bed for an indeterminate amount of time. The first couple of weeks I was so exhausted I pretty much just slept. When I finally was able to stay awake for longer intervals, I became frustrated because there were so many things I wanted to do, but couldn't.

Each morning, I tried to convince myself that this must surely be the day that God will raise me up. As I reiterated the promises God had imparted to me before this trial, I wondered what He was waiting for. It didn't make sense that I had already been down for an entire month. There was too much to do. Besides, I didn't have any sick time benefits, and I needed to get back to work to earn some income.

One morning, as I was rehearsing all I should be accomplishing, I saw a vision of a banquet table covered with a white linen table cloth. Spread across the length of the table was a veritable feast. I heard in my spirit: *"I have spread a table before you. Feast on what I have given you."* The Lord then reminded me of Christian music and teaching CDs with which I had been blessed, as well as shelves of inspirational books. It was time (since I had lots of time) to feast on the bounty before me.

I would begin everyday asking God what I was supposed to listen to or read. I was amazed how He set before me exactly what I needed to feed my spirit. As I devoured the truths of God's Word through books and teachings, a deeper understanding and healing began to take place in my heart. Layers of hurts, I thought I had already dealt with were removed, and God began to stir up the testimonies He had already given me, many of which I am sharing with you in this book.

Although most days I would have clear direction as to what I was to feast upon, there were days when I wouldn't have a clue. It was very common on those days for someone to come and visit; often they had a gift for me. Once, it was a stack of teaching CD's about destiny that had been purchased at a yard sale. Sometimes it was a book, an article, or a small token to remind me that God loved me and that He had a purpose for my fiery trial. I never knew in advance how God would prepare my table, but each day I heartily feasted on the delicacies that were spread before me.

One particular delivery stands out in my memory because it involved a very unusual messenger. Early one morning, as I lay on my bed inquiring about my next spiritual meal, the Lord told me to go and see my neighbor Alicia.

"Go see Alicia?" I questioned out loud, "Making it down the hall is a huge feat in itself. Why on earth would God want me to go all of the way across to the next apartment? Maybe I am getting it backwards. Maybe Alicia is supposed to come see *me*. After all, she daily comes over to check on me anyway."

But as I picked up my cell phone to call, the Lord assured me that instead of Alicia coming, I was to be the one to go. There was no rhyme or reason to it, but I obediently called and told her, "Open your door because I'm coming over—and I'm in my jammies!"

I slid off my bed and carefully made my way down the hall to my living room where I collapsed on the couch. Then after resting for a few minutes, I reached over, opened my door, set my sights on Alicia's doorway, and mustered up my courage and strength. One, two, three... go!

I cleared the breezeway within seconds and as soon as I was safely through the doorway, I collapsed in her living room chair. With my head over one chair arm and my legs dangling over the other, I waited until I caught my breath. Then I nonchalantly asked "So, how is everything going?"

After giving me a quizzical look, Alicia simply replied, "Fine."

"Is there anything you need prayer for?" I asked.

Alicia peeked over the top of her reading glasses, laid her knitting down in her lap and gave me one of those, *What is Jeannie up to now?* looks. "No, not anything I can think of."

She then picked her yarn back up and resumed her knitting, while I continued to lie across the arms of her chair staring at her with a confused look on my face, feeling dumber than a rock. I told her the Lord had instructed me to come over, and I didn't have a clue why. Since she had no clue either, we chatted a little as I watched her granddaughter Meagan play on the floor.

After a short visit, complete with a performance of *Jesus loves Me* sung by the adorable two-year-old, cherub-faced child, I decided that I must have misunderstood something and thought it might be time to go back home. But in my spirit I still felt that there was a reason for my being there.

As I was gathering up strength to get out of the chair, Meagan disappeared into the next room and came out holding a book in her hands. At first, I didn't pay much attention to the book she was shoving toward her grandmother, but then my eye caught the word "Heaven." I thought to myself, "No, it couldn't be." I asked the child if I could see her book.

Sure enough, when she held it up, I realized it was the very book a few of my friends had told me they felt the Lord wanted me to read since I was currently grieving the death of a dear friend. I had a hard time containing my excitement as I explained to Alicia about the book. She said that she had bought it that very morning, and I was welcome to read it first if I liked.

That day, I took home another portion of God's feast with great delight. Not just because of the confirmation that I was supposed to read the book, but because of the *way* God had orchestrated getting it into my hands. I knew if He could put together the circumstances to place that book in my hands from the hands of a toddler, He could put together the circumstances to bring forth my healing and fulfill the vision He had placed in my heart.

♥ Heart Encounter ♥

1. The way that God put the book about Heaven into my hands reminds me of the anointing of Saul in 1 Samuel chapters 9 and 10. Read about the chain of events that God orchestrated in order for the divine meeting between Samuel and Saul to take place. When God orchestrates something, He doesn't leave anything out. He can use the simplest or the most complex circumstances to fulfill what He has declared. Describe the incredible events that had to come together in order for Saul to be anointed.

2. There will be periods in our lives when you and I will be faced with difficult challenges. In those times, when we don't know what to do, we need to keep in mind that the Lord our Shepherd is willing and able to spread a table before us in the presence of our enemies. Whether those enemies are actual people, or circumstances, such as sickness, financial challenges, and disappointments, we can feast on what God has given us. What are some of the difficulties that you are facing right now?

3. My mother set a wonderful example of this. Due to encephalitis, she was in bed for extended periods of time when I was growing up. But instead of allowing her enemy, sickness, to overcome her and hold her captive, she touched the world from her bed. I guess you could say that she had a mattress ministry. There was rarely an occasion when I would go in her room and not find her either reading her Bible, encouraging people over the phone, or writing letters. Consequently, there were some soldiers in Vietnam, as well as many state side citizens, who were encouraged that God loved them, and that there were people who appreciated them and cared about them. Can you think of a time when God birthed ministry in the midst of your adversity? Explain.

4. There is a song I used to sing that is based on Song of Solomon 2:4. "He brought me to the banqueting house, And his banner over me *was* love." Do you believe that it is God's love that brings you to the banqueting table?

Rarely are the circumstances (In my case they ended up being mercury toxicity and adrenal issues) that bring us to the table what *we* would have chosen. Remember, the table is spread in the midst of our enemies. Realizing that there are some delicacies that nourish our souls and enrich our spirits that are only available in adversity will encourage us to not only persevere but to gloriously overcome. So if you are currently in an uncomfortable place, realize that there may be a reason for it. Not only is God able to bring you through your trial by orchestrating whatever circumstances are necessary, He is also perfectly capable of spreading a banqueting table in the midst, at which you can feast.

Let's Pray:

Precious Lord, I am so very thankful that, as in Psalm 23:5, "You prepare a table before me in the presence of my enemies." When I am surrounded, you not only minister to my spirit, but you also orchestrate opportunities in my adversity. Open the eyes of my heart so that I can see the table in the midst and feast upon all that you spread before me. In Jesus' Name…Amen!

Reflections:

_____
_____
_____
_____
_____
_____
_____
_____
_____

The Tale of Three Beds

When I moved to an apartment that had a "no water bed policy" I was forced to give up my gentle waves for a couple of worn mattresses on the floor. My sleep was fitful as I would toss and turn throughout the night, trying to find a position to relieve my aching back and hips.

Although I toyed with the idea of asking around to see if I might find something *better*, I decided instead, to be grateful and *settle* with what I had. After all, I reasoned, there were so many people in the world who had so much less.

Each morning, as I would drag my tired, sore body out of bed, I would beg God for the energy and strength to make it through another day. Then I would tack on a short prayer asking for more restful sleep and relief from the pain that racked my weary frame.

One day a friend surprised me with two more mattresses. "Aha!" I thought to myself, "This is the perfect solution!" I rejoiced in answered prayer and hurriedly stacked the mattresses on the ones I already had. "God, you are so good to me!!!" I exclaimed as I climbed up on my new bed. From my new perch I felt like a mixture between a princess and an eagle. That night I slept better than I had slept in a very long time. And when I awoke in the morning feeling refreshed and in less pain, I once again celebrated the goodness of God.

Although I loved the better sleep benefits, there was just *one* catch to my "princess bed." Although it was much softer than my previous arrangement, with the slightest wrong turn, the mattresses would tip, causing me to topple to the floor. I initially had to participate in a precarious balancing act in order to stay upright. But with some training and a great deal of creative maneuvering, I soon managed to keep my bed stabilized the majority of the time.

Unfortunately, my darling children couldn't snuggle with me anymore because of the precariousness of the situation, and as all children will, they decided to take advantage of the opportunity. Sometimes, when I was peacefully reading or relaxing in bed, my ruffians would rush into my room and amidst squeals of laughter they would leap up and topple me to the floor, mattresses and all.

Although I tried spreading out my arms and grabbing the edges of the top mattress in an attempt to stay upright, I still ended up on the floor, so I decided just to laugh with my children and enjoy the ride. Besides, I was willing to deal with a *few inconveniences* in order to feel like a princess, even if it meant keeping up my guard.

One day, a friend approached me with an urgent request. There was a single mother with small children who were sleeping on the floor. "Would you give them two of your mattresses?" he asked. A cold chill went up my spine, unfortunately not out of compassion for the little children, but because the thought of giving up the comfort of my bed was distressing. "Sometimes my children *like* sleeping on the floor," I reasoned to myself. "Besides, this is the best bed I have had in a long time. Surely God would not want me to give it up. I just can't let it go! After all, am I not learning that I am His princess?"

However, with the passing of the next few days, my heart became more troubled, until, I finally knew what I had to do. Reluctantly, I called my friend and told him to come and get two of the mattresses. Although, I felt as though I had plummeted from my perch, I knew I had given up my comfort for a worthy cause, which at least made the decision more bearable.

A short while later I received a tax refund that was much larger than I had expected. I thought of all of the things that I could do with the money, including save it for future bills. But the more I prayed, the more I felt like I was supposed to take a large portion of it and buy a bed—and not just any bed, but a brand new queen-sized bed. As I began to shop around, I soon realized that new beds cost a fortune. Thus, the battle began. How on earth could I justify spending such a large amount of money on myself?

By this time, I had learned to receive gifts. So I could have accepted a bed if it had been a gift. But to make such an expensive purchase when there were so many needs in my family seemed preposterous. Once again God was dealing with my shame and poverty mentality, and as usual, I didn't want to go there. But the Lord and a good friend kept pushing me forward until I agreed to go shopping.

As I lay upon the various mattresses, I felt a little like Goldilocks in the story of *The Three Bears*. Some beds were too hard like Papa Bear's bed and some were too soft like Mama Bear's bed. However, lo and behold, I eventually nestled down into a bed that was *just right*. The pillow-soft foam cushioned my weary body, and I felt absolutely *no* pain. I was elated! What made things even better was that the bed was on sale!

My friend and I went to the bank, I withdrew money, and I returned to the store to purchase my "Baby Bear" bed. But when I stepped out of the car, unworthiness cloaked me like a shroud, causing me to stand still in my tracks. The voice of the enemy screamed in my head, "You don't deserve that bed! How can you be so selfish?" I asked my friend to pray for me. Then I literally had to force myself to take each step as I fought against the enemy's onslaught by repeating, "I am a daughter of the King, and He wants what is best for me!"

As soon as I paid for the bed, the Lord's peace enveloped me, and within a few days my bed was delivered. Once it was set up, I immediately laid down. The comfort and luxury overwhelmed me as I nestled into the pillow-top foam. I thought to myself, "So this is what it feels like to be a princess—comfortable, spoiled, safe, and secure!

When I was sleeping on two worn mattresses I was in constant pain and was sleep-deprived. Although there might have been a better solution, I convinced myself, I could bear my current circumstances, so I became comfortable with the uncomfortable. I didn't even try to look for something else. Later when I was blessed with two more mattresses, I thought I had found the perfect solution. But when I gave up what I understood to be best, something much better was waiting just around the corner.

Often times, you and I settle for much less than God intended because we are either deceived into thinking that we are not worth more or that there is nothing better, or we are unwilling to let go of what we know. In order to try to sustain comfort or a sense of security we create solutions in our own understanding—solutions that often cause us to participate in precarious balancing acts that deprive us of blessings or even cause us harm. When we put our trust in the Lord and come down from our self-made perches by letting go of what *we* know to be best, we will often find that God has *His best* waiting in the wings.

♥ *Heart Encounter* ♥

1. Although God wants us to be thankful, He does not want us to settle. There is an interesting story found in 2 Kings 13:14-19 in which King Joash is given instructions after shooting an arrow to declare God's victory over his enemies. Joash is told to strike the ground with the remaining arrows, but he only strikes the ground three times. In verse 19 Elisha angrily tells Joash, "You should have struck five or six times; then you would have struck down Syria until you had destroyed it. But now you shall strike Syria down only three times" (AMP). Joash settling for less than God had planned for him cost him. Can you think of a time in your life when you settled for less? What were the consequences?

2. Many times, you and I settle because we see ourselves as *less than*. This can be devastating, especially in the area of relationships. Do you see yourself as being *less than* or do you believe that you are valuable and deserve God's best? Why or why not?

3. I used to think what I deserved was based upon my behavior and my circumstances. I now realize that God always desires to give me His best—just because

I am His child. It's not about what I have or have not done. It is solely because of what Jesus has already done for me. I always have God's favor, but many times I must align my life with His Word and His promises in order to receive His blessings. Do you believe that you have to earn God's favor or do you believe that God wants what is best for you, just because you are His child?

4. When you and I are deceived or in pain, we often will accept something that looks a *little* better as our solution. A great illustration of settling is found in Genesis chapter 16 when Abram and Sarai (later to be renamed Abraham and Sarah) tried to bring about the fulfillment of their promised future descendants through Sarah's handmaiden. The result was a precarious balancing act that is still continuing in the Middle East today. Can you think of a time when you came up with a solution of your *own* understanding that eventually backfired? Give an example.

5. Often when we give up the very thing we are holding onto in fear of not having better, the best is waiting just around the corner. Is there anything that you are holding onto that could be keeping you from God's best? It could be possessions, a job, where you live, a ministry position, or a relationship. It could even be a

mindset or attitude that you have adopted. Ask the Holy Spirit to reveal what you need to let go of so you can be ready to receive God's best.

Although we are to be thankful and content with what we have, we should not always accept all of our present circumstances as necessarily being God's best. It's easy to get comfortable in our circumstances or even in our "Christian walk." Sometimes we have to get rid of the old so we can embrace the new. If you and I are using all of our own strength and understanding trying to *hold on*, it might be time to *let go* and let God bring us wisdom concerning His best. However, as in my situation, we must be willing to move in the *opposite* direction of our understanding in order to take hold of our blessing.

Let's Pray:

Dear Lord, I am so grateful I am your child. That makes me royalty! Thank you for all of your blessings! Reveal any areas in my life where I have settled instead of believing for and receiving your best. Help me to trust you and to let go of anything that might be hindering me from embracing all you have for me. I love you Lord! In Jesus' Name...Amen!

Reflections:

_____

_____

_____

_____

_____

_____

_____

_____

More

*W*hen God told me to get out of bed and lay face-down on the floor a particular morning in 2003, I had no idea I was getting ready to have a Moses and the burning bush experience (minus the burning bush). But the Lord spoke so strongly in my spirit I had no choice but to listen. *"Like Moses, you are to deliver my people from Egypt. I want you to start a single's ministry"*

"Ummm, singles ministry?" I countered. "But Lord, I never *wanted* to be single! Besides, I can't speak. I don't believe in women teaching men. And did you forget? Right now I hate men!" I was sure my statements would disqualify me. But instead of letting me off the hook, God promised to equip me as He lovingly replied: *"I know. I will help you. And I am going to break your heart for men the way I have broken your heart for women."*

From past experiences, I had learned not to say "no" to God, so I did the next best thing—I agreed to pray about it.

Call me cautious (or terrified), but six months later when I attended a ladies' retreat in Tucson, I was still "praying about it." I had already talked to my pastors, who had thrown a wrench in my plans to abandon ship when they excitedly said, "We have been praying for someone to lead the singles!" However, because of fear and insecurities, and a good dose of stubbornness, I was still waiting for further confirmation to move forward—or better yet—withdraw. That confirmation came from a stranger who prayed for me at the retreat "Whatever God has told you to do," she instructed, "God says, 'Quit praying about it and just do it!'"

So I did!

Once I stepped out in faith and began a singles' Bible study, God stepped in and amazingly changed all my "I can'ts" into "I can do all things through Christ who strengthens me" (Philippians 4:13). As the Lord's strength was perfected in my weakness, I learned to both lead and teach. I also read numerous books about and for men, and developed healthy male friendships. As I heard the men's hearts and witnessed their struggles, God fulfilled His promise and broke my heart for men the way He had for women.

There used to be a popular expression in Charismatic circles that said, "There is more on the floor." Little did I know when God told me to lay on the floor that morning in 2003, that I would receive not only more than I wanted to imagine, but as in Ephesians 3:20, more than I ever could have thought or imagined. Although I had originally resisted God's plan to lead single Christians, the blessings I received during that particular season as I bonded, battled, prayed, played, grew, and healed with my siblings in Christ were definitely more than anything I ever could have imagined.

I love the phrase, "God does not call the equipped; He equips the called." I was both terrified and clueless when God first called me to lead Christian singles. And to be honest, our first few meetings were—let's just say—*Interesting!* It took a lot of prayer, perseverance, time, and divine intervention to get the group going. But although it got off to a rocky start, God met us and grew us along the way.

I thank God for His direction, equipping, and faithfulness. I didn't *get it* at first, but there was definitely *more* the morning He met me on the floor.

♥ *Heart Encounter* ♥

1. Have you been given direction for your next season or your life's calling? If so, are you moving forward, or is there something holding you back?

2. Read Exodus chapter 3. Do you think God knew Moses' weaknesses when He called him to deliver the

Israelites? Does it encourage you to know that God knows your weaknesses? Why or why not?

3. God is not concerned about our inadequacies; He just wants our trust and obedience. I recently read about a man with a great ministry who held a seminar teaching others how to grow their ministries. Throughout the entire seminar he taught one message: I prayed and I obeyed. Are you praying about something God has put on your heart? If so, have you obeyed?

4. Maybe, you are praying the thing to death like I was. Although God was faithful to bring me a word of confirmation, He had already confirmed my direction both in my heart and through my pastors. Looking back, I think I was hoping that God would forget. Have you ever felt that if you just waited long enough, maybe God will forget or choose someone else? Are you in that place now?

5. What are some fears that might be holding you back? What are some of the blessings you might miss out on if you don't step forward?

I wasn't trying to be rebellious when God directed me

to start a Christian singles group. I honestly *didn't* think I was capable of teaching or leading. It also didn't help that I had a deep distrust of men from being hurt. But none of that disqualified me. I realize now that my fears were linked to pride. After all, isn't it pride to think that you and I know more about ourselves and our abilities than the One who created us?

Thankfully, God sees beyond our inadequacies. What Moses thought he was incapable of doing eventually became second nature to him. I used to think I was incapable of teaching Bible studies, but now writing and teaching studies is second nature to me. We might not understand when God calls us to step into something new, but we can be confidently assured He knows what He can and will do in us and through us when He calls us to *more*.

Let's Pray:

Dear Lord, I am so very thankful that the plans you have for me are not based on my abilities, but on your capability. Forgive me for my pride, and help me to trust you. Teach me how to pray and obey so I can move forward into the great adventure of the *more* that you want to do in me and through me. In Jesus' Name....Amen!

Reflections:

_____

_____

_____

_____

_____

_____

_____

_____

_____

A Matter of Life

$\mathcal{A}$ single question kept turning over in my mind as I mechanically rocked back and forth in my rocking chair. "Why now?"

My husband Joe and I reunited after having been separated for three months while he was changing jobs and relocating to a new state. Since we had communicated very little while we were apart, and I had dreaded our reunion, his cordial greeting when the children and I met him at the airport caught me off-guard. It also gave me a tiny glimmer of hope concerning a possible new beginning.

Although being together again still felt uncomfortable, the atmosphere in our home over the past couple of months had become less intense, and we had recently been engaging in some short, shallow conversations. I had begun to get encouraged about the future of our marriage and our family—but not any longer.

An interruption in my monthly cycle had compelled me to get a pregnancy test, so earlier in the morning I had paid a visit to the local crisis pregnancy center. I wasn't sure what to expect when I pulled into the parking lot of the small establishment, but as soon as I walked in the door, I felt love. I was immediately encouraged by the welcoming smiles and heartfelt compassion of the volunteer staff.

While anxiously awaiting the results of my test, my mind had shifted back five years before when I found out I was pregnant with our firstborn. Although we had not planned on having children right away, the red plus sign on that home pregnancy test had signified otherwise. "How should I tell Joe?" I thought. "He will be sooo excited!"

As I thought about how I would announce the *wonderful news* of our first born, a story I once heard came to mind. In the story, when the wife finds out that she is pregnant she decides to surprise her husband by knitting baby booties in front of him. Although it takes a while, when he realizes he is going to be a father, he takes her in his arms and declares, "You have made me the happiest man in the world!" I couldn't help but smile as I thought about how elated Joe would be when he found out that we were expecting our first little bundle of joy.

I had to chuck the baby bootie idea because I didn't know how to knit, so I did the next best thing. I went to the bookshelf and grabbed *I Should Have Seen it Coming when the Rabbit Died* by Teresa Bloomingdale. I couldn't help giggling as I positioned myself so my hubby could easily read the cover when he came in the room. As I excitedly waited for Joe to declare, "I am the happiest man in the world," I mentally rehearsed the chorus of Paul Anka's song *Having My Baby*. "Hmmm. I wonder how long it will take him to *catch on*?" I mused. Just when I thought the waiting was going to kill me, I heard the doorknob turn.

Joe was quite perceptive and caught on quickly. And he did burst—but not with joy. His exact words were, "This is the worst thing that has ever happened to me. I wish I could crawl in a hole and die! You know what I believe! You know what you can do about it!" Since abortion had not been unfamiliar to his family and friends, I knew exactly what he was implying.

After his outburst he left, slamming the door behind him. I laid in shock trying to let it sink in, while rehearsing what had just transpired. My dream crushed, I found myself swirling in a whirlwind of emotions and questions. What was I going to do? Was abortion an option? Although I had heard for years that abortion was wrong, all of the sudden, it didn't *seem* quite so wrong. My baby and I had just been rejected by the person who was supposed to care for us the most. Was I being forced to choose between my baby and my husband, and if so, which one would I choose? How could I choose? Could ending the pregnancy eliminate the friction between us? Besides, is a month-old fetus really even a baby?

As the questions occupied my mind, pictures from an anti-abortion pamphlet a stranger had given me in college came to the forefront of my thoughts. The long-forgotten, bloody, mutilated images that I had conveniently turned my head from a few years before, now loomed before me in a desperate hour, speaking truth and putting an end to my questions. The life growing inside of me was not just a blob of tissue. It was real. It was valuable. It was a baby! No matter what the outcome, this baby would be here to stay.

After three days of our home having been shrouded by a veil of silence, the tide slowly began to turn. Joe accepted the fact that we were going to be parents, and he began to look forward to the birth of our baby. The pregnancy was challenging for both of us, financially, physically, and spiritually. But even in the midst of our doubts about provision and fears concerning my health and our future, God moved so mightily that it was unbelievable. We not only were blessed with everything we needed, but I received an incredible miracle in my body which *gave me back my life.*

"But that was five years ago. What about now?" I thought to myself, as I sat in the waiting room of the center. Our oldest son was now in kindergarten and we also had two beautiful daughters—one three years old and the other eight months. I didn't think I could handle another baby, especially since Joe's angry outbursts kept us all walking on eggshells most of the time. But I couldn't think about all that now. I just needed the test results.

The minutes ticking by seemed like hours. I studied the photographs of the mothers proudly holding their newborns that adorned the walls. Some of them had seemed incredibly young, some much older. Each had her own story that had been woven at some point into the tapestry of this small but fruitful clinic that was ministering love.

Off to the side, I had observed racks and racks of maternity and baby clothes just waiting to be gifted to expectant mothers. Directly behind me was another small room stocked with car seats, strollers, and cribs. "What a beautiful ministry!" I thought to myself, "How I wish more women would know about it." Momentarily, the loneliness I had been feeling began to lighten as I realized that there were people who not only understood and who truly cared, but who would be there for me as they had been for other mothers and their babies.

That is when a soft, kind voice pulled me back to the present. As I looked into the smiling face of a precious middle age woman standing in front of me, holding out my test results in one hand while clasping a tiny pair of knitted baby booties (how ironic) in the other, I realized that my greatest fears were being confirmed. I was definitely pregnant. My heart sank as I had thought about the difficulties that lay ahead.

All of that was just this morning. It seemed like so much in such a short while. Now here I sat in my living room waiting, just waiting—thinking—and rocking and waiting.

As I turned the small variegated booties in my hands, numerous scenarios played through my head as I thought of ways to avoid the wrath that was surely to be coming my way. Although I had no fear of physical harm, I just didn't think I had the strength this time to crawl out from under the heap of condemnation and accusations that would certainly be hurled upon me. Besides, I wasn't exactly happy about the test results either. Even though Joe was in the home, I was pretty much raising the kids alone. My quiver was full, and I was exhausted. The last thing I wanted was another baby to care for. I would have four children under six years of age. "My hands would be full, but my life didn't have to be miserable," I said aloud, "Why don't I just do it without Joe?"

I began to think about escape options. Maybe I wouldn't say anything and just leave with the kids without any explanation. I would wait until I was a thousand miles away and then tell my husband the news. It would be much easier through the disconnectedness of the phone line, and besides, I could just hang up or hold the phone far away so I wouldn't get hit with the onslaught of angry words. Or maybe I would wait until the baby was secure in my arms. That would be easier. If I left and waited eight months to place the call it would be a sure-fire way of eliminating any innuendos to abortion. No matter the choices, my current situation seemed pretty hopeless.

After weighing all of my options, I made the decision

to *get it over with* and just tell Joe upfront. Sure enough he reacted as I expected. Not only was it *my fault* that our birth control wasn't effective, he actually made it sound as if he hadn't even been part of the conception. Then after delivering his verbal barrage similar to five years before, he took off, slamming the door behind him.

That is when I got angry—really angry—angry at the whole horrible mess. I stomped into my room and began to pace back and forth as I boldly declared to God, "How could you let something like this happen? We were just starting to get along! Besides, my body hasn't even recovered from the last one!"

There have been a few times in my life when I have heard the voice of the Lord resounding in my head with such intense volume it seemed to be almost audible. This was one of them: *"Only I can create life! Do not give Satan the credit!"* The words reverberated through my brain with such intensity I stopped in my tracks. Then I felt led to read Genesis 30. After looking up the passage and reading about how God opened and closed the wombs of Rachel and Leah, I heard, *"I am adding to you another son."*

"Why Lord? Why now? Why this way? A baby delivered to my door would have been so much easier. Besides, this is terrible timing. I can't handle two in diapers again!" Then my focus changed from my situation to the cases of others. "Okay! Then what about the unwed teenage mothers who seem to spit out one baby after another?" I questioned. "And how about my friends who have been trying to adopt a baby? Why can't couples who want children have them, when so many who don't want them get pregnant?" No matter what scenarios I laid out, God's mind didn't change. He didn't explain to me the "whys" behind everything, but He did make it very clear that *He* creates life and that a child is *always* a blessing. If someone is *blinded* to the blessing or chooses to *destroy* the life and *miss* the blessing, it doesn't *negate* the fact that God *created* the life and *gave* the blessing. I left my room that day with a new understanding of pregnancy and life in general. Children are *always* a blessing. Even if we are blinded to the gift temporarily, they are always a blessing!

♥ *Heart Encounter* ♥

1. I had to come to the realization that both my husband's and my reactions stemmed from fear, selfishness, false beliefs, and social influences. It breaks my heart that we, as a society, have taken the blessing out of birth, and given ourselves the right to decide the value of each child. What does the Bible say about children?

2. In Psalm 127:3 the Bible tells us "Behold, children *are* a heritage from the Lord, the fruit of the womb *is* a reward." Do we prize or disdain rewards?

3. One morning, when I was praying about the abortion issue, the Lord brought to my attention how in the Old Testament children were often sacrificed in the worship of false gods. What idols are calling for the sacrifice of our children today?

4. A young woman called me one evening and asked if I would meet with her and her pregnant friend. We set up a time for the following morning. Early the next morning, I felt a grieving in my spirit and as if I was being ripped apart. Not long after, I received a phone call. Apparently, that morning her friend had decided to talk to a counselor at a pro-choice facility. When the facility discovered she had planned to talk to a Christian, they convinced her to have an immediate abortion. I had been feeling the death of the baby in my spirit. How much more do you think that the Lord grieves when His "little ones" are destroyed because of lies, fear, and greed?

5. In Genesis chapter 30 we see a twisted web of deceit and manipulation as two women are competing for the

love of one man. (Just more proof that monogamy is a very good thing.) But even in the midst of the mess, God in His mercy and love chooses to bless and give the gift of life. As you read the chapter, notice how many times it says, "and God listened." Who opened and closed the wombs?

There are so many "whys" you and I would like to ask God; for some of them we won't have the answers until we get to heaven. But it only makes sense that since God creates life, the devil would want to destroy it. Over a million women are deceived into getting abortions every year. I could have easily been one of them. Instead of condemning women who have had abortions, you and I need to grieve for them and help them heal. Often they are the other silent victims in their stories. We need be aware of the deception of the abortion industry and condemn the lies of the enemy denouncing the precious lives that God has created.

There is healing at the foot of the cross for those who have had abortions, encouraged abortions, participated in abortions, or lost a child they "couldn't save" from an abortion. There was (is) also instant healing in Heaven for the babies who have been (are being) aborted. Although these precious babes are safe in Jesus' arms, we will never know the loss this world has experienced, because each and every baby was surely meant to be a blessing.

Let's Pray:

Sweet Jesus, thank you that you are the healer, the deliverer, and the restorer of broken lives. Forgive us individually and as a nation for the millions of precious lives that have been devalued and destroyed. Show us the deception and selfishness in our hearts that would cause us to sacrifice our sons and daughters. Give us compassion for the wounded women and men who bear the scars of abortion as we stand in truth and acknowledge and reject the lies of the enemy. Touch our hearts and lives with what touches your heart and help us to always embrace life as a beautiful gift from you. In Jesus' Name...Amen!

Reflections:

_____

_____

_____

_____

_____

_____

_____

_____

The Cave

When I was in my late twenties, God gave me a word to prepare me for the coming New Year. At the time I didn't realize it would be a yearly tradition, but after the first few years I came to expect it. Usually, it was a just a short phrase like, "Rest in My peace," or "New beginnings," or "This year will be a roller coaster ride." But the word He gave me on New Year's Eve of one particular year was not only longer than any other I had received, it was perplexing.

After scrawling out more than a page and a half of sentences preparing me for triumph in the midst of tragedy, I was not just confused, but concerned. "Lord, what's this about? I thought we were in restoration," I inwardly voiced.

I soon found out. Five minutes after midnight, I received some traumatic news that sent me reeling. The Lord had known that I would desperately need His words to sustain me during the following months! "How could something like this happen to someone I loved so dearly—someone I had tried to protect? Where was God? Why did He allow this to happen? How had I failed?"

As the questions ran through my head, I ran into the other room and fell to floor feeling utterly abandoned.

Deep sobs wracked my frame. My hopes lay shattered as I rose to my knees, looked up, and cried out in anguish: "I tried to do everything you asked of me! Where are you God?! 'My God! My God! Why hast thou forsaken me?!'" As the words passed my lips, I almost couldn't believe I had dared to speak them. Surely God would chastise me for being so irreverent—so bold.

God's voice was silent, but His heart was not. Immediately, I saw a vision of Jesus hanging on the cross calling out to Heaven. As He cried those very words in the midst of His suffering and anguish, Father God turned his head. In than instant, with every fiber of my being, I knew that because Jesus was forsaken, I never would be. Although I didn't know how we were going to make it through, I knew the words I had written on New Year's Eve were true. Someway, somehow, God would bring triumph out of tragedy, and good would come forth from the devastation. My God would *always* be there for me—no matter what.

The next morning, although I was still in emotional turmoil and pain, I had a glimmer of hope. As I sat in the living room re-reading the words of the previous day, I saw a vision of a cave. Although the first part of the cave was expansive, the farther I walked, the narrower the passages became. I groped my way along in the darkness, trying to find the next opening. As the crevasses narrowed and moved closer to the floor, walking turned to creeping and eventually crawling. I forced my body through a final crevasse and crawled into an enormous room that was illuminated by supernatural light. Gold and jewels adorned the walls, and unspeakable treasures lay in heaping piles on the floor.

I knew the Lord was showing me that I was heading into a difficult, dark season. It would be so difficult that, at times, I would feel as if I would not be able to make it. Circumstances would arise that would drain me so much they would put me on my face and force me to crawl. Although, it would be hard, and I might not understand, in the end there would be incredible treasures—treasures that would be illuminated by His glory.

I won't go into the details of that year, but I will tell you, I have *never* experienced more confusion and pain. There were days when I was curled up in a fetal position. I had to force myself to get up and keep going. Often during that season of consequences, confrontations, investigations, and temptations—mainly for revenge— my prayer was: "Lord, we're not going to make it! You have got to do something!" Little did I know that He already was moving on our behalf; I just couldn't see it at the time.

No matter how dark and how difficult the journey, my Heavenly Father never left me nor forsook me. He walked with me, and sometimes carried me each step of the way as He comforted, encouraged, and guided me through the "cave." Along the way He gave me great treasures of deeper intimacy with Him, greater love for others, rich testimony, and future ministry to the hurting and hopeless.

I now see the treasures more than the passages of the cave. Although I couldn't imagine a new day when I was in the midst of my pain, I can truly say that the Lord has turned my mourning into dancing and my sorrow into joy.

♥ Heart Encounter ♥

1. In Matthew chapter 5 we are promised that God "comforts those who mourn." He also "draws close to the brokenhearted" (Psalm 34:18). Do you believe that God is there for you no matter what you are "going through"—even when you may not *feel* it?

2. When I was going through my "dark season" God kept giving me the scripture, "Weeping may endure for a night, But joy comes in the morning (Psalm 30:5b). At the time I was grieving I couldn't even comprehend "joy," and sometimes "the morning" seemed like it would never come. But eventually, the dawn broke and a "New Day" did begin. Are you or

someone you know currently in a "nighttime" season that seems like it will never end? Explain.

3. Isaiah 61:3 tells us that God gives us "beauty for ashes," "the oil of joy for morning," and the "garment of praise for heaviness." It's His promise. It's His heart. This scripture reminds me of a photo a friend once sent me. It was of a beautiful field of flowers that had sprung up from the ashes of a devastating forest fire. Do you believe that God can and will bring forth beauty from the ashes in your life? Explain.

4. One of the ways the enemy kept tormenting me was by telling me I failed by not protecting. Another way was the horrible pictures that kept playing in my mind. The issue wasn't whether or not I had failed, the issue was whose voice was I going to believe: the voice of the devil condemning me, or My Father's voice promising me that He was more than able to "work all things for good." In order to break the torment, I had to take both thoughts and images captive, pray the blood of Jesus over my mind, and claim God's promises. If you are being tormented by condemnation and/or horrific images, what are some of God's promises that will help you break off the torment?

5. God draws close to us and comforts us through His presence and through the people He has placed in our lives. I personally don't know what I would have done had I not had the support of some of my family and friends. What kind of support system do you have?

If you are going through a season of confusion and pain, know that the Lord loves you. He feels what you feel, and He is there to comfort and guide you. Although it may not seem like it now, as you press into Him, He is amassing great treasures. "I will give you the treasures of darkness And hidden riches of secret places, That you may know that I, the Lord, Who call *you* by name, *Am* the God of Israel" (Isaiah 45:3). So hold on, my friend. Wail, shout (even at God), do whatever you need to do to turn to Him and face the pain. Just keep pressing into Him and, like me, someday you will be able to see His glory revealed when He brings forth triumph in the midst of tragedy and restoration out of the devastation.

Let's Pray:

Sweet Lord, sometimes life hurts so much it's difficult to find words. Thank you for always being there for me—even when I don't feel it. Jesus, because you were forsaken, I am drawn close. Because you were forsaken, I do not have to walk alone. Because you were forsaken, all the devastating things that have happened will be turned for good. Thank you for taking my place so I will never be forsaken, even in the darkest seasons in my life. I love you, Lord! In Jesus' Name...Amen!

Reflections:

_____

_____

_____

_____

_____

_____

_____

_____

_____

The Chariot

I can still picture him today: sandy brown hair, dimpled cheeks, perfect teeth, and big brown eyes. He was attractive, wealthy, athletic, and popular. But regardless of everything Charlie had going for him, his sole purpose in life seemed to be to torment others. *I* just happened to be on his hit list.

Racism was obviously Charlie's motivation for bullying Ted, a little black boy from Trinidad, but I was at a loss as to why he picked on me. Maybe it was because, as some say, bullies have built-in radar that hones in on insecurity. No matter the reason, it was agony sitting through fourth period English.

Our 7th grade teacher, a sweet little white-haired granny, seemed oblivious to the daily drama that played out in her classroom. Intermittently throughout fourth period, Charlie would turn around and make degrading sexual and grotesque remarks to Ted and me. Ted would defend himself by responding likewise. But I countered

Charlie's incoming artillery the only way I knew how to—through silence.

I vowed that I would not let Charlie "get to me." Instead I would just ignore him and smile. Not only did it anger him when I refused to react, it also gave me a warped sense of satisfaction knowing that he was unaware of my façade. For beneath my smiles was gut-wrenching pain and lots of shame, and I often felt as if I were drowning in a torrid flood of perverse filth and degradation.

When Charlie couldn't rile me verbally, he began to take more assertive measures to torment me, like once when he tripped me when I was using crutches. I had torn ligaments in my ankle from a fall out of a tree. The subsequent fall from being tripped, caused further injury to my torn ligaments, extending recovery time to over a month. It also further damaged my weakened spirit.

I should have confided in my parents, but since they were continuously battling the aggressive outbursts of my special needs sister, I decided to carry my anguish deep inside, where it ate away at me like a slow cancer. I would smile my way through the intense situations during school, and then retreat home angry and depressed. Hidden away in my room, I would try to escape the pain by entertaining morbid thoughts—even thoughts of suicide.

I wasn't aware of it then, but looking back, I realize that the Lord met me many times that year, including the afternoon a vision of loved ones in heaven caused me to put down the knife I was getting ready to plunge into my chest. Although I told no one of my torment, God provided a way out for me when one of my sisters came forward and told Mom and Dad how she was being bullied and showed them the death threats she had received. As a result, three of my siblings and I were enrolled in a private Christian school the following fall.

I loved my new school! It was free of drugs, violence, and bullies. Feeling safe gave me the opportunity to come out of my shell a bit and trust my teachers and establish new friendships. However, when my parents were informed that the Christian school wasn't accredited and that a new principal had brought about necessary change at my former junior high, they decided to put me back in public school. So in the middle of ninth-grade I tucked myself back into my protective shell and returned to my old campus, my old friends (I think I had two) and my bully—Charlie.

The new school staffing had brought about many positive changes, including much less violence. Charlie still treated me with disdain, but thankfully, he never outright verbally or physically attacked me again. Life on my old turf was bearable. I finished ninth grade uneventfully and proceeded to high school the following fall.

I was still painfully shy and insecure when I entered high school, but in hopes of a fresh start, I enrolled in a few extracurricular activities. Little by little, I began to emerge from my protective shell. By my senior year I could answer questions in class without shaking, walk through the halls without staring at the floor, and make eye contact without feeling I would shrivel up and die. I even sang a solo in our student body's talent contest. My painful years were now behind me!

Charlie attended the same high school, but he was not in any of my classes. Except for the rare occasions when I would catch a glimpse of him walking across campus, as far I as was concerned, he didn't even exist—that is—until one day near the end of our senior year. I had stayed late after school for a musical rehearsal. Not a soul was in sight as I hurriedly collected my books from my locker. The eeriness in the echoes of my footsteps caused me to quicken my pace. I slowed considerably as I approached the double doors leading to the parking lot when I noticed someone standing on the other side. It was Charlie!

Fear immediately gripped me! I wasn't sure if I should retreat or advance. I mustered my courage and moved forward. As I forcefully pushed the bar on the inside of the door, Charlie grabbed the outside handle and pulled the door open the rest of the way. He held the door for me, his face registering a soft almost humble expression as he managed a weak smile. He seemed almost timid. With a voice just above a whisper he said, "Hi."

His unexpected greeting had the effect of a bullet tearing through my soul. The festering wound it struck dislodged a barrage of unspoken hatred. "How dare he?!"

I inwardly fumed. "After all of the torment he put me through, how dare he have the audacity to speak to me!"
I stepped aside, walked past Charlie, and went home feeling justified and victorious. I had finally conquered my bully! Charlie also went home. That night as I sat on the edge of my bed and said my prayers, he sat on the edge of his, pressed the barrel of a .45 to his head and pulled the trigger.

I was devastated when I heard the news of Charlie's suicide. And for years the enemy tried to convince me that I was responsible for his death. I now realize that I am only responsible for my own choices. Although I didn't choose death for Charlie, regretfully I also didn't lead him toward life. My own pain and unforgiveness blinded me to his pain, and I missed his cry for help. A cry that was masked in a simple "Hi" that was barely above a whisper.

Not long after Charlie died, I heard a sermon that stirred my spirit. My pastor compared the hurting souls who pass us by on the road of life, to chariots. The following poem was birthed in my heart through that sermon. I pray it will bless you.

The Chariot

I passed a chariot on the road
And turned as I went by.
His heavy burden I did not see
Nor for his pain did I cry.

So caught up in my own world
My heart didn't even break
As I went on my merry way
And he—his life did take.

Since then I've asked the Lord
To open up my eyes
To others who are hurting so
And make me realize:

That kind and caring words
Or a simple spoken prayer
Can sometimes turn the tide of choice
When someone's caught in Satan's lair.

Open your heart to the Chariots.
Yes, reach out and be a friend;
You might just see a beginning
When there would have been an end.

♥ *Heart Encounter* ♥

1. Are you being sensitive to the chariots around you?
   It's so easy to get caught up in the hustle and bustle of
   life or to be so wrapped up in our own pain or selfish
   and judgmental thoughts that we miss the heart cries

of the hurting. Read Matthew 9:36. What was Jesus' heart like toward people?

2. *Merriam-Webster's Online Dictionary* defines compassion as "Sympathetic consciousness of other's distress together with a desire to alleviate it." Given this definition, would you agree that true compassion spurs us to some kind of action? Why or why not?

3. Let's look at the story of the woman at the well in John chapter four. How did Jesus minister to this woman? What can we learn from His example?

4. John 4:9 reads "Then the woman of Samaria said to Him, "How is it that You, being a Jew ask a drink of me a Samaritan woman? For Jews have no dealings with Samaritans." Not only were the Samaritans and the Jews enemies, men in that culture weren't even supposed to talk to women. Why do you think that the Samaritan woman came to draw water at the hour she did?

5. I have heard some say that it was because the woman was not accepted well by her community, maybe even because of her reputation. Sometimes I find myself

holding an unwritten list of criteria that determines who I will befriend or with whom I will share Jesus. Can you relate? If so, what is on your list?

6. In my mid-twenties, God began to burden my heart for my neighbors. One of the first people with whom I began to study the Bible was a melodramatic red-head who talked like sailor, smoked like a chimney, and drank like a fish. She definitely would not have met my criteria. I saw a mess, but God saw a wounded daughter. If the Lord had not stirred my spirit to reach out to this precious woman, I probably would have walked away. How should we "choose" with whom we will share Christ?

I love reading the testimonies of men and women of God who have impacted others through the leading of the Holy Spirit! One such book is *The Cross and the Switchblade*. It is the story of David Wilkerson, the founder of Teen Challenge. David's Spirit-led prayers and simple obedience opened doors for God to move mightily among the gang members of New York City. Through his ministry, *Teen Challenge*, God transformed men and women full of hatred into vessels of His love, deliverance, and mercy to others. What if David would have been led by his own understanding and only shared Jesus with "safe people" instead of hardened criminals, some who even threatened his life? Would the *Teen Challenge* ministry, which is responsible for rehabilitating drug addicts worldwide, even be in existence? Thankfully, we don't have to find out.

Let's Pray:

Precious Lord, thank you for loving me and saving me. Heal me from my hurts and hang-ups and make me sensitive to your Holy Spirit. Move me with your compassion and break my heart for the lost and hurting. Erase any unwritten criteria I might have that hinders me from loving and being available to the chariots that daily pass by me on the road of life. I love you, Lord! In Jesus' Name…Amen!

Reflections:

_____

_____

_____

_____

_____

_____

_____

_____

It's You!

God loves everyone and wants them to know Him. He also knows their hurts, their struggles, and the condition of their hearts. That is why when the Holy Spirit nudges me to speak a word to someone, or to hear their story, or just to pray with him or her, I see it as a life-giving opportunity. Whether it's my seat partner on an airplane or a complete stranger in a grocery store I have come to treasure these opportunities or "divine appointments." But that had not always been the case.

I used to be so terrified to talk to strangers that I often questioned whether the nudges in my spirit to share Christ or give a word were even from God. One night I turned on the TV just in time to catch a speaker talking about witnessing. He said, "When the Lord leads you to talk to someone about Christ, don't question if it is God. Do you really think the devil would want you to tell people about Jesus?" This new understanding moved me into a new place. It was no more a question of *if* God was leading me to share with strangers, it was strictly a matter of *would I care enough* to obey His leading.

I decided to obey the nudges and witness, but my fear and rejection issues caused me to come up with a "safe plan." I guess you could call it my chicken-hearted, self-protective witnessing routine. It went something like this: whenever the Holy Spirit would zero me in on someone and tell me to share, I would first take note if they were alone. If they were, I would walk over to them and ask them how they were doing. Then I would tell them what God had put on my heart for them. Many times, it was simply, "Do you know Jesus? He loves you and has a plan for your life." But sometimes the messages were much more involved, even to the point of God revealing specific details about their lives or current circumstances in order to give them hope or bring them freedom.

If the person I was being led to talk to was not alone, I would stand at a distance and pray the following prayer: "Lord, if you want me to talk to this person, make everyone around him or her leave." Invariably, within minutes of my praying, the area, aisle, or table (depending where I was at the time) would clear, and the individual would be left alone. Only then, would I, *Miss Scaredy Cat,* approach the lone individual and share the "love of God."

My little routine had worked pretty well until one evening when I was shopping at our local department store. I was looking for some material to sew my daughters some dresses, and the counter was packed. As I perused the bolts of fabric, I felt the familiar nudge of the Spirit to talk to a middle-aged woman with short, dark hair who was standing near the register. So I quickly retreated behind the nearest shelving and began to pray my familiar liturgy: "Lord, if you want me to talk to this woman, have everyone else leave the counter." As soon I prayed the word "counter," I heard very strongly in my spirit: *"Not this time!"* Apparently, I was supposed to talk to the woman in front of everybody. I was terrified!

In reluctant obedience, I slowly approached the counter with as much confidence as a deer caught in headlights. I stood directly in front of the woman and asked her if she attended church somewhere. When she replied, "No," I invited her to visit the congregation to which I belonged at the time. I then asked her if she knew Jesus as her Savior. When she looked at me and again curtly replied "No, I don't." I froze. It was as if my mouth had been glued shut. I couldn't say a word. I just stood there for what seemed an eternity looking at the mixture of stupefied and smirking faces that surrounded me. I slowly walked away feeling both embarrassed and humiliated.

On the way home, although I kept apologizing to the Lord for *blowing it,* I couldn't stop praying. That night, every time I started to fall asleep, I would see the woman's face, and intensely cry out for her salvation. Somewhere, in the wee hours of the morning, I finally succumbed to a fitful sleep.

I awoke at dawn rehearsing the events of the

following evening. As I reiterated my inability to witness, the enemy screamed at me that I was a failure, and before noon, I had made a decision not to witness to strangers ever again—period!

Three years went by and I had held to my word. Although I continued to pray and shared regularly with friends and relatives, I avoided sharing with strangers at all costs. That is, until one particular Sunday morning. I had settled into my seat at church when I looked over and saw a female visitor. Since I had made it a point to meet new visitors, I wandered over a few rows and sat down beside her. She introduced herself as Janet. We began to engage in casual conversation in which I explained to her that I had just started attending church here a few months previously. When I mentioned the name of my former congregation, she looked me in the eyes and said, "I think I know you from somewhere. Did you used to have brown hair?" After I answered affirmatively, she continued, "Did you witness to a woman at the material counter three years ago?" My face must have registered surprise as I again answered, "Yes." Then, full of excitement, she began saying over and over again, "You're the one! You're the one! You're the one! I was that woman! I have looked for you everywhere!"

Apparently, when I had approached Janet three years earlier, she was into the occult. She was also suicidal. In her own words, "I was as close to death as a person can get." Ironically, I was the third Christian who had crossed Janet's path in two weeks. So when I had asked her if she knew Jesus, she told herself, "Oh great, I'm getting ready to be proselytized to again!" She had braced herself to reject what I was going to say, but then she told me, "You didn't say anything else. You just walked away." As she drove home she kept thinking to herself, "Is this Jesus calling me to be one of His?"

One night, two weeks later, Janet had a personal encounter with Christ. When she knelt down at the foot of her bed and asked Jesus into her heart, she was instantly delivered. Shortly afterwards, since she had wanted to tell me about her radical conversion, Janet went to my old church. When she didn't see me there (we were on vacation at the time) she visited another church the following Sunday. And that is where she had been attending for the past three years. Janet said the reason why she was sitting talking to me is because God had told her to come and visit this congregation that morning.

As she continued to share, she let me know that during the last couple of years she had looked for me everywhere she went, and that she was so excited she had finally been able to share her story with me. I then shared with her how the enemy had convinced me that I was a failure because I couldn't think of anything to say that particular evening, and that I hadn't witnessed to a stranger since. Needless to say, talking to her brought me to repentance and armed me with a new boldness.

♥ Heart Encounter ♥

1. It grieves my heart to think of the spiritual games I have played at times in order to satiate my pride and have man's approval. Do you ever find it difficult to tell someone about Jesus because you are concerned about what others may think about you, or do to you?

2. As we read the New Testament, you and I face the realization that sharing the Lord can and sometimes will bring hostility against us. There are many examples of New Testament Christians being beaten and martyred. The same scenarios daily occur in many countries around the world today. In Philippians 1:21 the Apostle Paul says, "For to me, to live *is* Christ, and to die *is* gain" What are your thoughts regarding this verse?

3. If you and I truly want to see others come to Christ, we cannot be so concerned about our lives or our reputations. Our hearts have to be broken over what breaks the heart of God. It breaks His heart when people are lost and dying in their sins. When you and I care more about the lost than we do about man's approval, we will automatically share the goodness of

our God. Has your heart ever been broken for the lost? Is it broken now?

4. The Bible says in Luke 6:45, "For out of the abundance of the heart his mouth speaks." Is the love of God and all He has done for you flowing out of your mouth from the abundance of your heart?

5. Many times in our work places, we do not have the freedom to witness to our co-workers. But I have discovered even in restrained environments, the Lord can and will set up divine appointments. I have seen it over and over again in my own life, as well as in the lives of others. God knows how to bring people to us. The question is—when He does, will we be ready?

6. It's easy to get distracted in just doing life. That is why we must purpose to pray, read the Word, and listen to the leading of the Holy Spirit. Sometimes, we will just be led to pray silently for those around us, but at other times, God will give us instructions as to what we are to do or say. Are you daily setting yourself apart to be an instrument of the Lord? If so, how?

My good friend LeAnne recently told me that a co-worker came up to her and told her about a dream that she (the co-worker) had the night before. LeAnne was actually in the dream. This girl's dream opened the door for LeAnne to talk to her about the love of Jesus. If you haven't already, ask God for divine opportunities to share His love with others. You may be surprised how He puts them together. All you have to do is be a willing vessel. He will orchestrate the when, the where, and the how.

Let's Pray:

Precious Lord, I want to be a vessel for you. It's so easy to get distracted and caught up in my daily routine. Stir my heart so that your desires will be my desires. Break my heart over what breaks your heart, and fill me with your love until it overflows and spills out upon those around me. Orchestrate divine appointments in my life so others can receive the good news of your forgiveness and have a personal relationship with you. I choose to be set apart for your purposes. Thank you, Lord. In Jesus' Name…Amen!

Reflections:

_____

_____

_____

_____

_____

_____

_____

_____

_____

How Great a Love

*E*xcitement began welling up in me. I had heard over and over again in my spirit as we drove toward the dock, "This is the boat ride, this is the boat ride. This is what you were praying for. This is the boat ride."

Before I had left on the mission trip to the Philippines, I, along with many others, had been led to pray for the people on the islands where we would be ministering. One particular morning I felt such a heavy burden to pray I could barely move. The Lord then spoke to my heart that instead of going about my normal routine, I was supposed to stay in bed and pray for the trip we would be taking by boat to cross over between Cebu and Negros. The longer I interceded, the more expectant I became. As vague, unfamiliar faces flashed through my mind, the Lord kept telling me He was going to move mightily on the boat ride. Two hours later, I finally felt a release, and I was able to get up.

During the following weeks, I read the mandatory

books about Filipino culture, prepared sermons, and gathered needed supplies for the trip. But no matter how much I learned or prayed, I still didn't feel any connection to the people. I truly wondered if I would be able to share the *love of God* instead of just the message of *His love*—whether on a boat or anywhere else.

However, when God tells us to go, He always meets us along the way and that is exactly what He did for me. There are no foreign people to the Lord. No matter the physical and cultural differences, we are all sinners in need of a Savior. We are all sick or wounded and in need of a healer. We are all precious in the sight of God, and He desires to touch *all* of our lives in a powerful way.

As our team went, our hearts were opened wide to God's heart, not only to bless, but to be blessed by the beautiful people of the Philippines. Amazingly, the Holy Spirit often gave us wisdom what to pray as we ministered in the schools, hospitals, and neighborhoods of the different *barangays* (small districts of the cities). Each time I stood in front of another person in the prayer line and divinely knew his or her physical and spiritual needs, I was overwhelmed with the love of God for that individual, and I was deeply touched in knowing that God had something precious to give them.

After only four days now into our journey, it was time to move on. They had been days filled with the pouring out of God's love, and I had been so blessed by the receptivity of the beautiful people of Cebu, I was dreading leaving. But now, in feeling the expectancy in my spirit concerning the upcoming boat ride, my sights were beginning to cast forward to the awaiting adventure. My whole focus turned to praying for the people that would soon be boarding.

Once our luggage had been loaded, we stepped onto a barge-like vessel and after walking the length of the cargo area, found ourselves in front of a small stairway. A short climb to the top revealed the lower deck. Being alerted that the trip might be a "little rough" motion-wise, our group decided to forgo the next set of stairs and positioned ourselves in the middle rows on the wooden benches. "Where are the people?" I thought to myself. "There is no one else here but us."

As I continued to watch the vacant stairway, minutes seemed like hours and doubts filled my head. Finally, I could hear someone coming up the stairs, but to my disappointment, it was only a middle-aged European couple we had seen standing by the dock earlier.

As they entered the seating area and moved over and stood by the railing, I began to rationalize, "I thought that there would be a lot of people on this boat, but there aren't, so maybe I misunderstood. Maybe instead, these two people will be like the apostle Paul and will reach many others. Besides, if they don't know the Lord, this is the opportunity for them to meet Him."

I slipped from my seat and walked over and asked the woman where she was from. She shook her head and declared in a loud thick accent, "I canna hear anyting! My ears topped up!" Both my countenance and my hopes fell, and I retreated back to my bench confused.

"God, where are the people?" I questioned. Then—they came. It seemed out of nowhere a steady stream of people began to pour from the top of the stairs until a constant flow of bodies filled not only the lower deck, but the entire upper deck as well. Many of them were high school students who could not only speak English, but who were also the one school group we didn't have the privilege to minister to in the *barangays*. Apparently, they had been on a field trip on the island and were now returning back home. The people kept coming until they were occupying the places that were for standing room only. My spirit leapt. I knew that God had placed them here for *such a time as this*.

Once we left the dock, our group began to sing a few songs, and the Negros pastor introduced us as American missionaries. When he sat down, his wife instructed me to get up and speak. I stumbled to and clenched the center post while being rocked back and forth by the waves. As I held on for dear life while attempting to keep my footing, I shared about the morning God had led me to pray while I was still in America. I told the passengers that they were not here by coincidence, but God had placed them on this boat at this particular time because He loved them and wanted them to know Him. As I studied their beautiful faces, my heart was enlarged. The revelation of God's love for others and for me that was placed in *my* spirit was so powerful I felt as if my heart literally would burst. After I finished testifying about how God had healed both my physical heart (in my mid-twenties God cancelled my surgery when He healed my heart murmur) and my emotional heart, I made my way back to my seat as the next person on our AGLOW team stumbled to the front to share.

When the invitation to accept Christ as Lord and Savior was given, almost all of the students prayed, and the majority raised their hands to show they wanted personal prayer. Since it was impossible to invite people up front for prayer because of the rough waters, our team members dispersed among the rows and sat next to a student on the end of each aisle. When we finished praying for the student on our left, we slid over them into the space they made and then prayed for the next student, until person by person and row by row, everyone received prayer.

Throughout the entire incredible experience I kept thinking, "Oh God! How great is your love! How great is your love!... A love that would stir hearts to pray... A love that would cross oceans and continents... A love that would put people, times, and places together with such precision... A love that reaches intimately into the heart of man... A love that knows all things and understands completely what is in each and every one of us...A love that desires to be known...Oh, how great a love!"

As I finish this book I pray that you would know that God has had you on my heart, and I have been praying for you as I have been writing. But more importantly, He has had you and always will have you on His heart. So if there is nothing else that you have received from these pages, may you close the cover knowing that not only are you on His mind, but that He loves you and adores you. May you continually open up your heart and life to Him and discover for yourself...*How Great a Love!*

God Bless,

Jeannie

Author's Note

(Concerning My Future Book)

A man recently sent me a heartbreaking testimony of severe abuse he received as a child. In his letter he commented, "I chuckle when I read or listen to experts of psychology or family counselors on either TV or radio when they say victims of abuse will, themselves, become abusers. When I was being abused, I resolved internally, with passion, to be kind and gentle toward people. That's who I am today."

Part of my reply was as follows:

God is good! As we all learn sooner or later in this life, hurting and deceived people hurt people. You mentioned that it makes you chuckle when people say that people who are abused grow up to be abusers. I personally have observed three main relational scenarios in people who have not been healed from being abused: 1.) The abused person becomes an enabler or continues to be abused when he/she becomes an adult. 2.) The abused person grows up to become an abuser. 3.) The abused person shuts down and isolates himself or herself. All three are consequences of a lack of knowledge, unforgiveness, denial, judgment, sin, and just a whole lot of pain. I have learned that people who abuse, and adults who allow others to abuse them, believe many of the same lies I used to believe about God, their value, and relationships—lies that keep them bound and keep them repeating detrimental cycles.

To that, he replied, "I am number three."

Most of our life stories contain at least two scenarios, if not all three. At one time or another, some of us have even played all three roles. That is why it is so important to learn truth and walk in freedom.

Thankfully, both abusers and abusees can become healthy and whole and break the cycle. I am currently writing a book about the lies that kept me in abuse. In the process I have created a survey, and I am interviewing women who are either currently in abusive marriages or have come out of abusive marriages. If you would like to participate in the survey, please contact me at truthrejoices@gmail.com. Your information will be confidential. If I do share part of your story, it will only be with your permission. Please join with me to break the cycle of abuse in the lives of men, women, and children! It's all about God's love! It's all about freedom! It's all about helping others fulfill their God given destinies!

God Bless,

Jeannie

ENDNOTES

References for "Trash"
Connie Williams, "The Wheel of Idolatry, Growth Group Ministries," Emmanuel Fellowship, Cottonwood, AZ

References for "Clearer Vision"
"My Eyes Adored You," written by Bob Crewe & Kenny Nolan, sung by Frankie Vali, Private Stock Records, 1974, 45003

References for "Betrayed"
Matt Redman, "Blessed Be Your Name," from the album Blessed Be Your Name: Songs of Matt Redman Vol. I (Sixsteps/EMI, 2005)

References for "A Table in the Midst"
Kevein Prosch "His Banner Over Me Is Love" (Mercy Publishing, 1991)

References for "Tale of Three Beds"
Arranged by Cooper Edens, Goldilocks and the Three Bears (Hong Kong, Green Tiger Press 1989)

References for "The Word Impossible"
Brother Andrew w/John & Elizabeth Sherril, God's Smuggler, Old Tappan, New Jersey Fleming H. Revell Company (Spire Books, 1967)

References for "The Chariot"
Meriam Webster's Online Dictionary-compassion.

David Wilkerson w/ John & Elizabeth Sherril , The Cross and the Switchblade, New York, NY, The Berkley Publishing Group 1962.